PLAYS THREE

For David Pownall

Torben Betts

PLAYS THREE

THE OPTIMIST
THE SWING OF THINGS
THE COMPANY MAN

Introduction by Adam Barnard

OBERON BOOKS
LONDON

First published in this collection in 2008 by Oberon Books Ltd.
Electronic edition published in 2013

Oberon Books Ltd
521 Caledonian Road, London N7 9RH
Tel: +44 (0) 20 7607 3637 / Fax: +44 (0) 20 7607 3629
e-mail: info@oberonbooks.com
www.oberonbooks.com

A catalogue record for this book is available from the British Library.

PB ISBN: 978-1-84002-824-9
E ISBN: 978-1-78319-421-6

eBook conversion by Replika Press PVT Ltd, India.

Contents

INTRODUCTION

The three plays in this volume are set in the houses and gardens of middle-class English homeowners. If this resonates security, my advice to the reader is: brace yourself. Just behind the tapestry fabric curtains, around the corner from the flourishing sunflowers, Torben Betts offers three assemblies of deeply pained human beings who struggle with the most basic questions about how we should live our lives.

This is a world of floundering, sub-Alpha males and suicidally miserable women, of bullying parents, torturous childhoods and failing relationships. These are lives wracked with despair over choices made, baffled by the most basic conundrum: what would it take to make me happy?

Each play in isolation is an assault on the image of modern England as a country where family, a little disposable income and 'good old bricks and mortar' (William's increasingly hollow catchphrase in *The Company Man*) are the supposed circumstances of happiness. Together the plays form both lament and manifesto. Betts elevates to protagonist status a procession of characters who are coming to terms with their own insignificance, pushed by circumstance to articulate their sense of talentlessness and failure. The urgency of their need to feel that 'there must be more to life' is crucial to these plays' dramatic potency.

A gathering of family or old acquaintances is the catalyst. Such occasions are all too often subsumed in stock-taking of your life and comparison with other people. Their successes stalk you as the ghosts of what you might have been. Unwittingly, yours do the same to them. Lives are reduced to measurements and the terms of success controlled by the strongest personalities; Donald's assumption at the beginning of *The Optimist* is that happiness is proportionate to house size and salary. The obtuse pressure of these sorts of parties is a burden; no surprise, then, that it is all too easy to misjudge a moment and find yourself publicly embarrassed.

And modern life itself is a burden. Witness Lindsay's obsession in *The Swing of Things* with buying her daughter a horse and getting her 'into that school', and the financial and psychological mess her husband Mark creates in the face of those aspirations. Mark, like Tom in *The Optimist* and Richard in *The Company Man*, retreats back into alcoholism to escape bankruptcy, both financial and emotional. The daughters in the latter two plays both turn their backs on England in favour of remote and unfamiliar countries where they can escape Western pressures and assumptions.

The plays echo each other not only in theme but also in theatrical language. Tense silences that 'build and build', a duologue where one party remains stubbornly mute, a confession from the heart during which the intended auditor slips away unnoticed, the awful embarrassment of overhearing what you are not meant to overhear, the inability to interject in what is supposedly a conversation, or even to finish a sentence – all are characteristic of a dramatic universe where nothing is easy.

So what genre is this work? *The Swing of Things*, which riffs on the dreaded school reunion, looks most obviously a comedy. Yet in a post-show discussion at the Stephen Joseph Theatre, the audience expressed surprise when an actor referred to 'playing comedy'. 'Is it a comedy?' someone asked. Someone else: 'I felt uncomfortable laughing. It was nervous laughter.'

And here I think is the particular genius of Betts, a dramatic vision for dissecting middle England which is truly his own. A drama of middle-class life in this playwright's hands is one of painful realism rather than glossy naturalism. Such is the seething uncertainty of the characters that the audience comes to share the mantra many of them adopt: 'I just don't know what to do.'

This is important because Betts is too often filed, especially by lazy critics, next to his sometime patron Sir Alan Ayckbourn, and latterly too with Mike Leigh. Ayckbourn's work nails the foibles of middle England to ingenious comic effect; Leigh's finds, in the minutiae of everyday life, something both sad and redeeming. But for all the surface similarities, what Betts offers is different and deserves to be assessed on its own terms. Played properly, these works should evoke in us the same anxiety that courses through the veins of their characters. This is not a theatre of carefully managed trajectories. These are characters who are either already in freefall as the play begins, or who find themselves hurled suddenly off the cliff towards its end.

Nor is this a theatre of existential despair. For all the pain of the characters, for all the discomfort of an audience watching them, there is huge thirst for life here. When the question, 'what have I done with my life?' is asked again and again with such urgency, life itself is elevated to the highest level.

The plays in this volume should be a rallying cry. As Lindsay comments in *The Swing of Things,* we are living longer than ever before. Many grow up facing a bewildering array of options. The mantra of our age, at a time when a few appearances on a TV gameshow constitutes 'making it', is that anyone can achieve anything. All you need is a bit of that elusive thing called talent. The hangover from this sunny, origin-shattering optimism is that it is increasingly difficult to pronounce yourself satisfied with your lot. For Richard, in the *The Company Man,* whose stab at pop stardom went nowhere, or Mark, the also-ran footballer of *The Swing of Things,* the age of opportunity is also the age of failure.

Redemption, then, lies in our relationship with time. Much of the suffering in these plays stems from characters' inability to free themselves from a negative obsession with the past (or, as with Caroline in *The Swing of Things* or Ben in *The Optimist,* constant projection into the future). 'Forget about the past,' Cathy advises Jane in *The Company Man.* 'But you see,' Jane replies. 'That's such a hard thing to do.' Moments later the play lurches twenty years into its own past to track the neglected spark between Jane and her adoring friend James, an opportunity for happiness missed because neither could bring themselves to seize the moment and run with it.

Our time is precious and finite, says Betts. That this is a godless universe is casually implicit. What emerges from these twisted, tortured scenarios is the importance of making the most of every moment. In the stammered words of Steve, the traumatised Gulf War veteran in *The Swing of Things*: 'I think the only people who really… appreciate this life…the wonder and beauty of this very short, precious life of ours…are people who've nearly lost it.' Later, appealing to Ruth to see the purpose of remaining alive, he offers a vision for a new life together: 'We'll just…be.'

Herein lies the universality of these plays, set among the detritus of comfortable lives in one of the wealthiest countries in the world. The more sophisticated our social structures become, the harder it is to remember the fundaments of the life they have been built around. Six-storey townhouses and six-figure salaries will never be a substitute for love.

Adam Barnard
Scarborough, 2007

THE OPTIMIST

Characters

DONALD
mid-50s, sometime lawyer,
now with a promising political career

ELAINE
early-30s, his partner,
heavily pregnant, lacking confidence

IAN
30s, Londoner, a burglar

BEN
23, Donald's son, a solicitor

CATRIONA
25, Donald's daughter, an aid worker

TOM
mid-50s, her partner and colleague

The action takes place at Donald and Elaine's recently acquired and very desirable North London residence.

It is the evening of Saturday 3 November 2001.

The stage is divided into three areas. Raised as high as possible at the back is the roof terrace, dominating the audience, while the front area of the stage is divided into two – the larger area being the living room, the smaller area the garden, in which there is a swing, almost hidden by undergrowth. The kitchen window looks out onto the garden. There is a door to the kitchen and a fire door onto the roof terrace. There is a high wall to the side of the garden area.

The Optimist was commissioned by Alan Ayckbourn and the Stephen Joseph Theatre in April 2002. At the time of going to press it had yet to receive a full professional production.

Act One

PROLOGUE

It is dusk. Darkness in the house and in the garden. We see a figure (IAN) appearing at the top of the garden wall at the side. He is holding a torch. He furtively looks around and then shines the torch over the house and garden area. He drops down off the wall and into the garden. He lands with a crash and a curse. He has a shoulder bag. He surveys the scene. He turns and carefully approaches the kitchen window and the door. He peers in. The window is open. He tries it. It opens wider. Suddenly security lights are activated, illuminating the garden area. He makes a frantic movement away from the house and back towards the wall at the side. He tries to leap back up and grab the top of the wall. He fails.

SCENE 1

The roof terrace, lit by floor lights.

DONALD stares out front, whiskey in hand, surveying the extensive view of the city afforded by his new property. After a while ELAINE, who is heavily pregnant, comes onto the roof. She watches him for a while.

ELAINE: I just wanted to tell you something: I'm really happy.
DONALD: (*Briefly turning round, smiling.*) I'm glad.
ELAINE: And it's because of you. The fact of you. In my life. Despite all that's happened. I really think we can start to get on with our lives again now.
DONALD: Yes.
ELAINE: And I really feel…just…happier.
DONALD: So do I.
ELAINE: And this house is so wonderful. Thank you for it. (*A pause.*) Are you coming down soon or…?
(*A long silence as he stares out.*)
I'm sorry. About earlier. Of course you're anxious. Who wouldn't be?
DONALD: I just feel I should have been there.
ELAINE: You're a busy man.
DONALD: Far too busy.
ELAINE: And her mother was there, wasn't she, so…

(*A long silence. He looks at her. He then looks out front again.*)

DONALD: I always dreamed of having a view like this. Living with this kind of perspective.

ELAINE: You really are the king of the castle now. You sure you don't need a coat?

DONALD: It's been a tough old time. A tough few months.

ELAINE: (*A weak laugh.*) A tough few years.

(*He drinks.*)

Listen, I wanted to ask you if…

DONALD: So how's the food coming along?

ELAINE: My first ever supper using my own Aga. It's rather sad I suppose but I've been looking forward to it all day…

DONALD: So, what are we having?

ELAINE: Caramelised pork in stout with what I hope will be…

DONALD: Sounds delicious.

ELAINE: (*A nervous laugh.*) Oh, but you're very kind.

DONALD: (*More serious.*) No. You're the one who's…kind.

(*He stares out again. A long silence.*)

It's just…awful. We could have lost her.

ELAINE: I know.

DONALD: Mary sounded upset. She sounded very upset.

ELAINE: But I suppose she was lucky. Compared to the…

DONALD: And she has a new 'friend' in tow apparently.

ELAINE: Well, that's…

DONALD: (*A subject change.*) Anyway…how are *you* feeling?

ELAINE: I'm fine. A bit nervous.

DONALD: It'll be fine. I've told you… Ben's a very affable…

ELAINE: And your daughter?

DONALD: I just don't know about her.

ELAINE: I'm sure she's going to be very loyal to her mother.

DONALD: Anyway they're adults now so… People's marriages end. People fall in love with other people. It's been happening since the dawn of time.

(*A silence.*)

ELAINE: I think he's ready to meet and greet actually.

DONALD: Definitely a girl.

ELAINE: I'm sure it's a boy.

DONALD: Boys are trouble.

ELAINE: And intellectually inferior.

DONALD: So true.

> (*They smile at each other.*
> *He then stares out at the view again. A long silence.*)
> A most pleasing panorama, is it not?

ELAINE: We should get one of those skyline maps. With all the landmarks. The silhouettes. The outlines.

DONALD: That would be…good. Definitely.

> (*A distant firework overhead.*)

ELAINE: Well, I'll go and get on then.

> (*She makes a move. A silence. She watches him looking out.*)
> You're still upset about the…the…the campaign?

DONALD: I am a little.

ELAINE: We do have to act, surely? It is our duty to act.

DONALD: A lot of people are going to die.

ELAINE: But you said yourself that in any war there…

DONALD: People who probably don't deserve to.

ELAINE: Donald, we can't just…do nothing. Let it all pass.

> (*A long silence. Then another firework.*)
> Enough is enough.

DONALD: I just don't know if we should be quite so bloody… slavish. So pugnacious.

ELAINE: I think that we have to present a united front and that's…

DONALD: Look, anyway…we don't need to talk about it tonight.

ELAINE: Stand alongside America and face these lunatics down.

DONALD: Let's try and be happy. For tonight at least.

ELAINE: At least?

DONALD: Just be happy that my daughter has come home from this wretched camp and…look, I really don't want to talk about it. This whole…situation.

ELAINE: You know you seem so…sad. Your eyes. Your eyes seem so sad.

DONALD: I've missed her. It's been a year. I just need to see her. (*He turns to her.*) You look lovely, you know.

ELAINE: Oh, I look like a great pudding.

DONALD: You don't. You look lovely. Blooming.

ELAINE: (*Laughing.*) Blooming awful, I should say!

DONALD: Mary…she always…both times…it seemed like it was a terrible trial. For her. For me. It was an inconvenience. I don't know.

ELAINE: But she was a wonderful mother and you…

DONALD: Well, maybe not an inconvenience. She was pleased but…at the same time…it was like me getting her pregnant was my way of holding her back or…

ELAINE: Well, she's certainly done more with her life than I have.

DONALD: She's a little older than you.

ELAINE: She's a woman worthy of admiration.

DONALD: Maybe.

ELAINE: She combined having a family with being a doctor and being politically active and she… And look at her now, she's still at the peak of her powers. Makes me feel like a dreary little homemaker actually.

DONALD: I think she thought that not pursuing a career was a betrayal of the cause. But we did suffer as a family.

ELAINE: But darling you were the one who…

DONALD: And then of course every weekend she'd insist on hauling the kids off to Greenham bloody Common…
(*A long silence as DONALD drinks.*)

ELAINE: Are you missing her? It's alright to. Thirty years is…
(*No response. He drinks. Goes back to looking at the view.*)
(*Cautiously.*) I don't want you to get annoyed or… Don't you think you might be… (*She breaks off.*)

DONALD: I am on tenterhooks, my darling.

ELAINE: I'm just a little bit worried about how much you're drinking. These days. That's all.

DONALD: Don't be. It's fine.
(*A silence.*)

ELAINE: Good. Okay. I'll…I'll go and get on then.
(*She exits.*
He drinks in silence.)

DONALD: Everything really is…perfectly fine.

SCENE 2

The garden.

IAN is on his feet. He looks around in a panic. Looks up at the wall. He is about to jump up again when:

ELAINE: (*Off.*) Excuse me!
   (*IAN turns around in a panic. He instinctively produces a nasty-looking knife. Then rethinks. Puts it away.*)
   (*Off.*) Could you wait a second, please?
   (*He looks around wildly, wondering what to do.*
   ELAINE appears at the door. She is wearing a Labour Party apron.)
   Listen, I've got your money. (*Sees it's not who she was expecting.*) Oh, where's...Darren? Has he gone home or...?
   (*No response.*)
   So you must be Mitch or Wayne or one of his myriad helpers?
   (*No response.*)
   So one can safely assume that you've finally finished this wretched wall?
   (*No response.*)
   Because this really has been going on for an eternity, hasn't it? And you've cemented in the glass now?
   (*No response.*)
   Now what about this wall here? Do you think anyone could climb over it? I mean, it's quite a drop. Do you think we should put some spikes up there too?
   (*No response.*)
   Or glass? I mean, do you think someone could actually climb over that?
IAN: (*After a pause.*) It's possible.
ELAINE: I suppose it is better to be safe than sorry. But these things are all so ugly, aren't they? Bits of broken beer bottles and metal whatnots. It's just so sad that we have to do all this in the first place.
   (*No response.*)
   Now I was...supposed to be paying Darren, I think?
IAN: You can pay me.

ELAINE: And you've definitely finished it this time?

IAN: (*After a pause.*) Yeah.

ELAINE: Right. So. Well, thank you for all your hard work then.

(*She hands him a cheque.*)

IAN: No good to me. We agreed cash.

ELAINE: Cash? I don't quite follow.

IAN: You know…cash?

ELAINE: I don't think that was made clear?

IAN: It's what… (*After a pause.*) …Darren said. He said two grand cash. Knock off five hundred for readies.

ELAINE: So…you agreed this with Donald then?

IAN: Keep the taxman well out of it, you know what I'm saying.

ELAINE: Well I'm not sure that I concur one hundred per cent with the idea of avoiding one's responsibilities.

(*An awkward silence.*)

IAN: When's it due?

ELAINE: End of next month.

IAN: Love babies.

ELAINE: Do you?

IAN: Cost an arm and a leg though, don't they?

ELAINE: Do they?

IAN: You know what flavour yet?

ELAINE: I beg your pardon?

IAN: As long as it's got all its bits in the right places?

(*A long silence.*)

ELAINE: I'll…I'll go and talk to him then. My partner. About the…

IAN: (*Looking out front.*) Great view.

ELAINE: Yes. We like it. We're…pleased. Delighted.

IAN: See for miles, can't you? The whole city. Top of the fucking world.

ELAINE: Yes. Good. (*After a pause.*) Quite. Yes. (*She leaves anxiously.*)

SCENE 3

The roof terrace.

DONALD is still staring out front. He drinks. A firework explodes overhead. After a time ELAINE appears behind.

ELAINE: The men doing the wall…they say you offered to pay cash.

DONALD: Have you had a look?

ELAINE: Well…no.

DONALD: Well, I think we should inspect the work, shouldn't we? Before shelling out?

ELAINE: But he does insist on cash. Says you agreed.

DONALD: Did I?

ELAINE: He'll knock off five hundred if you pay cash.

DONALD: Well…that seems reasonable enough, doesn't it?
(*A silence. DONALD continues to stare out front. He drinks.*)
Better get down to the old cash point then.

ELAINE: You're not seriously thinking about driving? It's only a short walk. Why don't you walk?

DONALD: Of course I can. Yes. And they've actually finished it this time? And cemented in the glass?

ELAINE: I assume so.

DONALD: There's always…things. To organise. Isn't there? In this tangled web of life we weave.

ELAINE: And we might have to defend the side wall too.

DONALD: Who says?

ELAINE: Mitch.

DONALD: Who's Mitch?

ELAINE: Darren's friend.

DONALD: It's so depressing to have to do all this. I mean, this is Highgate, after all.

ELAINE: Nick and Monica have barbed wire.

DONALD: (*Tory voice.*) To keep out the rabble, the bewildered herd, what?

ELAINE: Well…

DONALD: But, I suppose it is quite an old house. An old wall. A hundred and fifty years of wind and rain and what have you.

ELAINE: Well, we can't be too careful.

DONALD: Because it does block out the light a little down there. (*A pause.*) You know, I really do love this view.

ELAINE: I really think you'd better go and…

DONALD: Yes, yes, of course.

(*He continues to stare out front.*)

ELAINE: Listen, I'm sorry if I've been nagging again.

DONALD: You haven't. Really.

ELAINE: Really?

DONALD: I'm just tired and anxious. I don't mean to be grumpy.

ELAINE: You're not being.

(*They smile at each other.*)

But you *are* working too hard.

DONALD: I know.

ELAINE: We need to try and enjoy tonight. Forget about this …Afghanistan business and…relax. It's a big night for me.

DONALD: I know.

ELAINE: I do feel very nervous though.

DONALD: You're bound to.

(*A silence.*)

ELAINE: I put some finishing touches on the living room this afternoon.

DONALD: Then I shall have to give it a thorough inspection.

ELAINE: We might have to get someone else in though to finish the rest now because my back today was absolutely…

DONALD: Tradesmen in this country, they really do take the piss, don't they? They're idle, they're arrogant, they're not even proficient. I mean, when I think of the bugger who did the kitchen, the bathroom…

ELAINE: I know.

DONALD: It's as if they take some perverse pleasure in causing as much distress as possible. Motiveless maliciousness, I call it. Their little V-sign at what they perceive as the bourgeoisie.

ELAINE: Yes, that Irishman really was an appalling little shit.

DONALD: Christ… I sound like some old Tory from the
    shires…

ELAINE: Heaven forfend!

DONALD: I'd better hie me to the bank then…

ELAINE: Right. I'll tell him to…tell him to…
    (*DONALD has left.*)
    …tell him to hang on then, shall I?

SCENE 4

The garden.

IAN is waiting. ELAINE comes on.

ELAINE: My partner has just popped off to get your money.
    (*A pause.*) Sorry for the misunderstanding. I think he'll want
    to have a quick look at your work.

IAN: See you got a nice entry system round the front. CCTV.
    That to do with his work, is it?

ELAINE: Well, I mean, it's just standard…

IAN: Got enemies, has he?

ELAINE: Not really.

IAN: I mean, what do you have to do to own a place like this?

ELAINE: He's in politics actually.

IAN: Oh right.

ELAINE: Don't worry…he *is* one of the good guys.
    (*She laughs.*
    A long awkward silence.)

IAN: In the Government, is he?

ELAINE: Yes. He's involved with the M.o.D.

IAN: (*A laugh.*) He's a mod, is he?

ELAINE: (*Weak laugh.*) That's right.

IAN: Well, I didn't vote for him.

ELAINE: I suppose that's…that's your prerogative.

IAN: My what?

ELAINE: But we do live in a democracy and so…

IAN: All liars and murderers, in't they? When push comes to
    shove.
    (*A long awkward silence.*)

ELAINE: Well, if you'll excuse me…I'm in the middle of…

IAN: So…you like to cook, do you?

ELAINE: As it happens I do have a keen interest in all matters culinary, yes.

IAN: So…what's on the menu?

ELAINE: (*Nervous.*) Well…to start with I'm doing a parsnip and walnut soup. (*No response.*) Followed by some chicken liver pâté with Cointreau and orange. And I'm baking my own bread rolls actually. (*No response.*) And for the main dish I'm serving caramelised pork in stout. In Guinness. It's good old winter fare, I suppose. And that's with minted new potatoes, green beans and carrots.

IAN: Then what?

ELAINE: For dessert? Well, it's just a winter pudding really… served with a damson and sloe gin coulis.

IAN: Suppose it's important for when he's 'entertaining'. Having a bird what can cook.

(*A long awkward silence.*)

SCENE 5

The living room.

DONALD and ELAINE.

DONALD: It's just shoddy workmanship, that's all. He can't expect me to pay him for that. There's still gaps all over the place. And they've left all their rubbish down there. Their tools and everything. They haven't cleaned up at all! They can't possibly expect me to fork out when they've not done the job properly.

ELAINE: I think maybe you should just pay him the…

DONALD: I don't agree. Part of the reason this country…

ELAINE: I know, you said…

(*A silence. He looks at her.*)

DONALD: I'm sorry if I bore you, Elaine. I'm sorry if I go on.

ELAINE: No. It's just… I really need to get on with the…

DONALD: I just think they take the piss, they really do.

(*A long silence in which he sulks.*)

ELAINE: Oh please…don't sulk. What were you going to say?

DONALD: Not important.

ELAINE: I so want this to be a happy evening. I'm very keen that your children see a united front.

DONALD: They will.

ELAINE: It's important for me that they accept me.

DONALD: They're decent people. We brought them up to be decent people. And it goes without saying we also brought them both up to be good socialists.

ELAINE: I'm sure you…

DONALD: Which worked with one of them but I'm not so sure about the other.

ELAINE: All I'm saying is that they may well see me as the person who ruined their parents' marriage.

DONALD: Oh, you're hardly the scarlet woman, Elaine.

ELAINE: I'm not quite sure how to take that.

DONALD: Look, they know that we were unhappy, they're bright kids. And all they want is for Mary and I to start being happy again.

ELAINE: I know but…

DONALD: They are adult, progressive, modern young people.

ELAINE: I just want…

DONALD: One should never try too hard to be liked.

ELAINE: No.

DONALD: And that's sound advice. Now, what's this chap's name?

ELAINE: Mitch.

DONALD: I thought it was Dick or Dave or Dwayne…

ELAINE: It was Darren. He works with Mitch.

DONALD: Who's Darren?

ELAINE: The builder.

DONALD: That's Dave.

ELAINE: It's Darren.

DONALD: And who's Mitch?

ELAINE: He works with Darren.

DONALD: And what about Dave then? Where does he fit into this merry scheme?

ELAINE: There is no Dave.

DONALD: And Dick?

ELAINE: No Dick, no Dave, no Dwayne. There was a Wayne, I think, but…

DONALD: No Dick, no Dave?

ELAINE: No Dick, no Dave. Just Darren and Mitch.

DONALD: And Dwayne?

ELAINE: And Wayne.

DONALD: So where's Darren?

ELAINE: He's gone. So now it's just Mitch.

DONALD: Right then…lets see how this Mitch deals with a little bourgeois rebellion, shall we?

SCENE 6

The garden.

IAN alone. DONALD comes out from the kitchen.

DONALD: Sorry for the delay but…I couldn't find anywhere to park.

IAN: I saw your VW in the drive.

DONALD: Well, that's more my partner's car…I've actually just invested in a new Audi.

IAN: You like German models then?

DONALD: (*Laughing awkwardly.*) I wouldn't turn down a night with Claudia Schiffer.

(*The laugh peters out. A silence.*).

IAN: I'm in the wrong job.

DONALD: I did start out as a lawyer.

IAN: Oh yeah?

DONALD: Your average MP…as poor as a church mouse.

(*DONALD laughs. It peters out again.*)

I imagine you're wanting to see the colour of my money?

IAN: You imagine right.

DONALD: Well, I'm afraid you're going to be sadly disappointed.

IAN: Why's that then?

DONALD: (*A little nervous.*) Well…to be honest, I'm still not one hundred per cent impressed by the quality of your work.

IAN: I'm not leaving here without my money.

DONALD: But there's gaps all over the place, you've only cemented in about eight pieces of glass.

IAN: I want my money.

(*A long silence. A stand-off.*)

DONALD: Listen to me…you've stretched out what is essentially a simple bricklaying job to well over two months…

(*A long silence. A stand-off.*)

IAN: Give me a grand then.

DONALD: So…what I am saying is this…when you've done the job properly, and I'm hoping this will take you only a few more days, I will pay you what we agreed in full. I can't say fairer than that, can I?

IAN: I want the money.

DONALD: (*Laughing.*) And I wanted a straight wall with no gaps in it!

IAN: I'm not leaving.

(*A long silence. A stand-off.*)

DONALD: I'm not sure if your friend told you what I do for a living but I can have a team of security people here within…

IAN: So…just give me a grand then.

DONALD: (*Now swaying.*) I don't want to have a row with you but I've been taken for a mug a few too many times in the past by you chaps and, to be perfectly blunt, I'm just getting sick of it. We had two dreadful Irishmen in last month to strip our wooden floors and they left dust everywhere, all over the house. I mean, they hadn't even bothered to lay sheets. And when my partner asked them to clear it all up they just laughed at her. And she had to do it all herself. And as for these men who've just installed our kitchen they were late, they were unreliable, they overcharged outrageously and I'm just…You know? Enough is enough. That's all I'm saying.

IAN: (*Quietly, menacingly.*) I just want my money.

ELAINE: (*Off.*) Donald! Donald! (*Coming outside.*) Could you… excuse me, sorry… Mitch…maybe you could come and take a look at the pipes in the…

DONALD: What are you talking about?

ELAINE: There's water coming from the bathroom…it's quite
a trickle actually and it's coming down into the kitchen…
I think we need to call a plumber or…
(*A long silence. A stand-off.*)

DONALD: Christ.

ELAINE: I think we need to hurry. Really.
(*A silence as DONALD cogitates.*)

DONALD: I'll give you the money when you've fixed the
taps…

ELAINE: I think it's actually the pipes under the…

IAN: And I'll want paying for the plumbing.
(*A silence as DONALD cogitates.*)

ELAINE: Please, quickly. Thank you. This way. Thank you.
(*ELAINE leads IAN away.*)

SCENE 7

The roof terrace.

*BEN, in jeans and a rugby top, steps onto the terrace. He stares wide-eyed
at the view. He is holding a spectacular bouquet of flowers. DONALD
comes on behind him, with the drinks: another scotch for himself, a bottle
of lager for BEN.*

BEN: What an amazing house. And an amazing view. You can
see the whole city.

DONALD: I love to have a son that's pissed.

BEN: You're pissed. (*Pause.*) How old is it?

DONALD: Finished in 1859, I think. The man who had it built
had trading links with India. He was an ex-army bod who
moved into the tea trade.

BEN: Did well for himself out of it then?

DONALD: The English do like their cup of char, don't they?

BEN: (*Joke voice.*) Cuppa char!

BOTH: (*Joke voice.*) Cuppa char!
(*They laugh. It peters out.*)

DONALD: But she's certainly showing signs of her age.

BEN: Even so.

DONALD: The walls are crumbling to dust and it would appear that we've sprung some form of leak.

BEN: Amazing…

DONALD: Rate you're going you'll be able to afford something like this pretty soon yourself.

BEN: Hardly!

DONALD: Oh, you'll be a senior partner before you can say… I don't know…before you can say…'litigation'.

BEN: I wish!

DONALD: Well…I still think you're a born barrister.

BEN: Don't have the confidence.

DONALD: You're bristling with confidence.

BEN: Not like you. Not like that.

DONALD: Well, it's all an act.

BEN: I'm happy behind my desk.

DONALD: Well, you can always diversify.

BEN: Does get a bit dull on occasions…

DONALD: Everything does on occasions.

(*A silence.*)

Well, you're doing really well. What are you now, twenty-five?

BEN: Twenty-four.

DONALD: (*Handing him glass.*) You're well on your way. I'm proud of you.

(*They touch glasses and drink.*)

BEN: A phenomenal city, isn't it? When you see it from up here.

(*A silence.*)

So…where's the lady of the house then?

DONALD: She's attending to the…flood.

BEN: Course. Yeah.

(*A long silence. A distant firework.*)

DONALD: So…your sister then?

BEN: (*Mood changed.*) My sister.

DONALD: You went with your mother?

BEN: Yes. She's still in a bit of shock, I think.

DONALD: How many died?

BEN: Seventeen. Three children.

(*A silence.*)
To be honest, she's changed quite a lot. You'll maybe need to prepare yourself. For one thing, she swears a lot more than she used to.

DONALD: I said all along I didn't want her to go. I said all along that it was foolhardy and ill-conceived and… I mean…it's a wonderful organisation of course it is, but she's so…young and… I thought she could perhaps enjoy her innocence a bit longer before she… I mean, is she home for good now or…?

BEN: She'll tell you herself.

DONALD: And to think she was going to be a professional dancer at one point. Christ, if only she'd stuck to the bloody ballet.

BEN: She'll be alright, you know. She's a strong woman. Pretty determined.

DONALD: She's just like her bloody mother.
(*They drink. A silence.*)

BEN: (*Looking out at the view again.*) It really is amazing.
(*No response. They drink. A silence.*
BEN walks around the roof, looking over the railing.)
A fair old drop!

DONALD: Handy for when it all becomes too much.

BEN: I reckon you'd break a bone or two but it's definitely survivable.

DONALD: Not if you went head first.
(*They drink. A silence.*)
Is you mother okay?

BEN: She's worried about Cat but…

DONALD: In general, I mean?

BEN: Still overworked, I think.

DONALD: 'Twas ever thus.

BEN: You were both as bad as each other.

DONALD: (*Joke voice.*) It's what made this country great.
(*They drink. A silence.*)
Is she…is she seeing anyone, do you know, or…?
(*They drink. A silence.*)
You can tell me.

BEN: I'm not sure. She might be, Dad. I…
   (*They drink. A silence.*)
DONALD: We'll have to come back up here later. When the
   fun really starts.
BEN: God, yeah. It'll be…
DONALD: I'm told you can see almost every display in
   London.
BEN: Well…count me in.
DONALD: Always liked your Bonfire Nights, didn't you?
BEN: It's a strange ritual, though. Standing around fires,
   celebrating the execution of some Catholic nutcase.
DONALD: I suppose it is.
BEN: (*Joke military voice.*) On the other hand one does have to
   deal quite firmly with the Papists.
DONALD: (*Laughing.*) Don't let Elaine hear you say that!
BEN: She bats for the other team, does she?
DONALD: Fraid so.
BEN: (*Joke military voice.*) Well, we can't have that.
DONALD: Very uncomfortable about not being married. Very
   uncomfortable about having a child out of wedlock.
BEN: Should think so too!
   (*They laugh. The laughter peters out. They drink. A long
   silence.*)
   So I assume you've given up going to church, have you?
   Now that your mother and I aren't around to force…
BEN: (*After a pause.*) I go sometimes.
DONALD: (*Smiling.*) Liar.
   (*They drink.*
   DONALD becomes lost in thought.)
   Well, listen, I'd love to just…spend an afternoon with you
   at the football or go to the rugby and then sit in a pub or…
   Chatting. I don't know…it just seems… rather harder to do
   that. To find the time. These days.
BEN: Well, you're doing a difficult job, Dad.
DONALD: Yes.
BEN: And doing it really well…
DONALD: We must do it, though. You, me and your sister.
   Get together again. Get out into the country. Go for

a walk. Get out there. Into the fresh air. I so love the English countryside. Yes, we should take the car, plonk it somewhere and just…head off. And catch up. Properly.

BEN: Great. Sure. Any time.

DONALD: A deal?

BEN: A deal.

DONALD: Great.

(*A long silence.*)

You're not too…upset about your mother and I?

BEN: Well, no…it's sad but…it was coming for some time, I think.

DONALD: I still love her, you know. My best friend for thirty years.

BEN: Course.

DONALD: So… I just don't want you to…want you to… You know.

BEN: Don't worry, Dad. Really. I'm a big boy now.

DONALD: You certainly are.

(*They drink. A long silence.*)

I just don't want you to…worry. You just get on with your life. Enjoy being young.

BEN: I'll try.

DONALD: Because the time goes past bloody quickly, I can assure you.

BEN: Yes.

DONALD: So you just get on with your youth…and your… your brilliant young life.

(*They both revert to staring out front and drinking.*
We watch them for some time in their unease.)

SCENE 8

The living room.

ELAINE in the room, followed by IAN. He looks around the semi-decorated room.

IAN: That should hold it for a while.

ELAINE: Thank you.

(*ELAINE goes to a toolbox on the floor and opens it. She hands him a small saw.*)

IAN: I mean I'll sort it now but it's only temporary…advisable to lay new pipes. Complete overhaul.

ELAINE: Thank you.

(*A silence. They look around the room.*)

It's mediaeval style. I did a course in interior design about…

IAN: More to you than meets the eye, isn't there?

ELAINE: I'm not quite sure how to take that.

IAN: Take it as a compliment.

ELAINE: I just wanted to encapsulate the best of English design all through the house. All through the ages. There's a long way to go yet. We've got six floors.

(*He looks around.*)

(*Becoming more animated.*) The first thing I did was to paint the chimney breast and the walls either side and then I opened the little hearth here and made this fire surround from a railway sleeper. Found it on one of my walks actually. I then planed and stained it with a dark oak wax. I liberated these church candles from my uncle…who's actually a priest. Do you know Rolls and Rems?

IAN: (*After a pause.*) No.

ELAINE: They do this wonderful tapestry fabric which I've used around the window. And I'm rather proud of the pelmet up there. And then I cladded these walls with plywood and I treated the timber up there with the same wax I used on the hearth to create this panelling. And the coffee table, here. I actually converted this hideous thing that was left here with scaffolding planks, stained it with the wax and then screwed these studs into the top.

IAN: And how's the cooking going?

ELAINE: Yes, it's just…a slightly more sophisticated version of barbecued spare-ribs, really.

IAN: How do you get to live in a house like this?

ELAINE: Well, to be fair, my father was only a social worker.

IAN: Should see the shit-hole I grew up in.

ELAINE: As I say…

IAN: I mean, what are you people actually doing to own houses like this? Can't all be above board, can it?

ELAINE: Well, it's a lot of hard work, I suppose. Application. Commitment. Determination.

(*He begins to wonder around the room, inspecting things. He picks something up.*)

IAN: What's this?

ELAINE: Actually…

IAN: What's it for?

ELAINE: Actually I'd prefer it if you…didn't…

(*He puts it down.*)

…touch the…

IAN: No, well…I'd say all in all that you've not done a bad job.

ELAINE: Well, as I was saying, I did do a sort of course…a few years back and…

IAN: (*Picking up another object.*) What's this?

ELAINE: It's a rather expensive heirloom actually and so I'd rather you…

IAN: Nice.

ELAINE: As I say, I'd actually rather you…

IAN: Mind if I have a feel then?

ELAINE: Sorry?

IAN: Mind if I touch your…?

ELAINE: Well, I'm not sure…

IAN: You're beautiful, you know. Pregnant women. Absolutely beautiful.

(*A long silence.*)

If you'd rather not then…

ELAINE: (*Anxious.*) No. It's…it's fine. I suppose.

IAN: Sure?

ELAINE: Yes. Why not?

(*IAN approaches her and slowly, holds out his hand to her belly. He touches it. He looks at her. She looks away. It's both edgy and intimate.*)

IAN: You alright?

ELAINE: Yes, thank you.

(*A long silence.*)

It won't take you too long, will it? This pipework?

IAN: Shouldn't do.

ELAINE: Only I am…entertaining tonight.

(*With his hand still on her belly, they stare at each other for a time. She then looks away.*)

SCENE 9

The roof terrace.

DONALD and BEN in silence, looking at the view. A few fireworks overhead. After a while ELAINE comes on behind. An awkward silence prevails.

DONALD: (*Turning.*) Elaine! This then is my son and heir.

BEN: (*Giving her the flowers.*) I'm very pleased to meet you. At long last.

ELAINE: These are lovely. Thank you.

(*She proffers her face to be kissed, while he holds out his hand. Awkward moment.*)

BEN: You look nothing like the papers described you.

ELAINE: I'm sorry?

BEN: (*To DONALD.*) Journalists are such scumbags.

DONALD: Some of them certainly.

ELAINE: (*A nervous laugh.*) I'm not quite sure how to take that.

BEN: It's a wonderful house.

ELAINE: We're very pleased with it.

DONALD: Elaine's decorating the whole thing herself.

BEN: Really?

ELAINE: Well, not all of it. (*Pause.*) I did a course in interior…

DONALD: She can give you a guided tour later.

ELAINE: I'd love to.

BEN: Seems to have all died down a bit now, doesn't it? The press.

DONALD: (*Smiling.*) Yes, well they've sunk their teeth into some other unfortunates, I think.

BEN: (*To ELAINE.*) How was it for you, I mean…?

ELAINE: (*Very seriously.*) Absolutely horrible.

DONALD: Listen, I'm popping down for a top-up. Can I get anyone else anything?

BEN: Same again, Dad. Cheers.

DONALD: Darling?

(*ELAINE frowns at him.*)

Sorry, yes. (*Leaving.*) Bad idea.

ELAINE: (*Patting her bump, smiling.*) I'm off the alcohol of course.

BEN: (*Laughing.*) Of course.

(*A long silence.*)

Mild, isn't it? For November?

ELAINE: It is, yes.

BEN: Really mild.

(*A long silence.*)

It's an amazing view.

ELAINE: It's wonderful.

BEN: Civilisation.

(*A long silence.*)

ELAINE: So...how's the world of law and order?

BEN: It's fine, thank you.

ELAINE: It's corporate law, isn't it?

BEN: Correct.

ELAINE: Didn't fancy following in your father's footsteps then?

BEN: (*A laugh.*) What, divorces?

(*She laughs awkwardly. The laugh peters out. A silence.*)

We operate from offices in London, Edinburgh, Glasgow, Belfast, Paris, Frankfurt and Brussels.

ELAINE: Sounds...wonderful.

(*A long silence.*)

BEN: It really is an amazing view.

(*A long silence. A firework.*)

ELAINE: I'm sort of...nesting at the moment, I suppose.

BEN: That was a good one.

ELAINE: (*Laughing.*) Getting ready for the big life change.

BEN: Sorry, yes. Belated congratulations.

ELAINE: Bit nerve-racking...

BEN: (*Laughing.*) Rather you than me!

ELAINE: I'm a little apprehensive, I suppose but...

BEN: Bound to be...

ELAINE: But I'm sure it'll all...

BEN: And Dad tells me you're something of a wizard in the kitchen?

ELAINE: I do enjoy cooking, yes.

BEN: And what...what are we...I mean, tonight...is it...?

ELAINE: It's caramelised pork in stout.

(*A long silence. A firework.*)

BEN: Boom!

ELAINE: Yes.

(*He laughs. She laughs. A long silence. He smiles at her. The silence builds for a very long time until DONALD returns with the drinks.*)

BEN: Cheers, Dad.

DONALD: You've instructed that young-fellow-me-lad to fix the pipes then?

ELAINE: Well, yes.

DONALD: Is that wise?

ELAINE: I think it is an emergency, Donald.

DONALD: But he doesn't inspire me with a great deal of...

ELAINE: I can handle him.

DONALD: And he's going to charge the earth.

ELAINE: He says the piping's cracked, the water tank needs patching up and the stonework is all crumbling.

DONALD: I don't recall the surveyor mentioning any of that.

(*A pause.*) Well...on your head be it then.

(*A long silence.*)

BEN: Anyway, cheers.

DONALD: Cheers.

ELAINE: And...welcome.

(*BEN and DONALD drink. A silence. A firework.*)

SCENE 10

The garden.

CATRIONA is sat on the swing, looking sadly around her. BEN comes on behind. Neither speak for some time.

BEN: So...what do you think?

(*No response.*)

Lad's done well for himself, hasn't he?

(*A long silence.*)
So…where's your…friend?

CATRIONA: Buying wine.

BEN: Be a nice surprise for Dad, won't it?
(*A loud firework nearby. CATRIONA flinches slightly.*)
I just want to say, Cat…how much I admire you. What you've been doing. What you are doing.
(*No response.*)
I mean, I seem to have a life mapped out in an office, don't I? And I'm already pretty bored with it… You know, same shit different day and…
(*No response.*)
You know…you people…working in those camps…
Helping people. Saving people. I think you're just amazing. Really.
(*No response.*)
And I'm so proud of you.

CATRIONA: Can't actually believe they're doing this.

BEN: Who?

CATRIONA: It's…appalling.

BEN: What is, sorry?

CATRIONA: Bombing peasants. What have Afghan peasants got to do with any of this?

BEN: Well, I suppose they've got to flush Bin Laden out…

CATRIONA: Oh, come on…

BEN: The Americans do have a right to avenge themselves and…

CATRIONA: Do you have any idea how many people they're dropping their bombs on? Now. Right now. At this moment. People who are poor, people who are defenceless, people who have never hurt anyone in their whole fucking lives!?! Sheep farmers! Sheep farmers and their families!

BEN: Look, of course it's unfortunate if…

CATRIONA: Unfortunate!!?

BEN: But lets not talk about politics tonight.

CATRIONA: What else is there to talk about then? What else do people fucking talk about in their stupid fucking lives!

(*A very long silence, BEN shocked by the outburst.*)

BEN: Dad just wants to see you again. He doesn't want to fight about who's bombing who and the whys and the wherefores and…

CATRIONA: Our Government is colluding in mass murder and nobody…

BEN: Look, come on…

CATRIONA: The Americans have bombed Korea. China. Guatemala. Indonesia, Cuba. Vietnam.

BEN: Your list again?

CATRIONA: Laos, the Congo, Peru. Cambodia. El Salvador. Nicaragua. Grenada. Libya. Panama. Kuwait. Iraq. Somalia. Sudan. Yugoslavia.

BEN: This is your famous list then?

CATRIONA: And now Afghanistan.

BEN: We all know about your list.

CATRIONA: (*Tearful.*) Blair is a nasty little murdering cunt!
(*A very loud firework nearby.*
A very long silence.)
And so whatever happened to our dear old Donald? Not the man he used to be, is he?

BEN: Lets leave it tonight…

CATRIONA: As Mary says…

BEN: 'Mum', you mean?

CATRIONA: As Mary says…

BEN: What does 'Mary' say?

CATRIONA: Something went horribly wrong somewhere.

BEN: Anyway, listen, it's really good to see you again.

CATRIONA: Used to be my absolute hero. (*A silence.*) I really don't know what I'm doing here. I just feel so…so unhappy. I can't believe they're doing this.

BEN: Why take it so personally? Why carry the weight of…

CATRIONA: Because this is my fucking country! The people who represent me, who represent you, who are paid good money to represent me are committing a crime. A great big fucking war crime. And one of them is my father. And they will murder thousands of people over there and they won't bat a fucking eyelid, they'll all sleep like babies at night in their soft cotton sheets next to their fat fucking bitches with their big bank accounts and their big fucking five-storey houses in Highgate and then in a few years' time they'll go into Iraq and then maybe Iran and all for British business interests and American oil merchants and they'll murder thousands more and then, what a great fucking surprise, the murders will start coming home to us. The barbarian hoardes'll be blowing themselves up in Oxford Street, on the Underground, in the aeroplanes and then it's you and me, Bennyboy...it's you and me and not the liars and the cunts and the killers in Westminster who'll be left burnt and bleeding... Of course I take it fucking personally!

(*A very long silence.*)

BEN: You know, it's just so odd hearing you swear so much...

CATRIONA: I nearly died, brother!! Those fat fucking Jews dropped their fat fucking shells on the house where I was staying. A house full of fucking children! A house full of orphaned fucking children! And they did it with weapons they probably bought from our dear devoted old Papa!

(*CAT is now weeping.*
A very long silence.)

BEN: You never used to swear like this.

CATRIONA: Oh, Christ...

BEN: In fact, you never used to swear at all.

CATRIONA: A man with an education, with a good degree and you still haven't got a fucking clue!

BEN: Anyway, it's actually six storeys.

(*She gets up and walks away.*
DONALD comes on. Nobody speaks. He approaches her.
They look at each other. A tense stand-off.
He walks towards her and embraces her for quite a while, she hiding her tears.)

DONALD: I'm so glad you're home.

(*They eventually break from the embrace.*)

So...here we all there then.

BEN: Certainly are.

DONALD: The three of us.

(*A long silence.*)

BEN: It's an amazing garden.

DONALD: Not too good for rugby, though.

BEN: (*Laughing.*) Yeah…bit of a slope.

DONALD: Perhaps you…perhaps you'd like to come inside and meet Elaine? She's very…very keen to get to know you. Well…both of you.
(*DONALD looks to BEN again. He smiles sadly back.*)
So…your mother tells me you've met someone? That's… wonderful news. To have someone to help you through this difficult time. A friend. While you've been away from us? Maybe you could invite him round one night? We could meet him perhaps?

BEN: Sorry…Dad…he's coming tonight?

DONALD: I'm not…I don't quite follow.

BEN: He's here tonight. He's coming tonight.

DONALD: I don't think we were expecting him, were we?
(*A long silence.*)

BEN: Ah. Must have got our wires crossed. Sorry.

DONALD: Well, listen…we can always make room for a friend. No problem.

BEN: Should we tell Elaine or…?

DONALD: We can always…make room.
(*A long silence.*
CATRIONA looks towards her father.)
For a friend.
(*A few loud fireworks explode overhead.*)

SCENE 11

The living room.

DONALD and ELAINE.

ELAINE: (*In hushed tones.*) But I've only done the four pieces of pork!

DONALD: (*Likewise.*) You've only done…?

ELAINE: The four pieces of pork, yes.

DONALD: Well…

ELAINE: Why didn't you tell me?

DONALD: Ben and I…we seem to have got our wires crossed.

ELAINE: This is so embarrassing.

DONALD: I don't know if…

ELAINE: I am absolutely mortified.

DONALD: Look, he can have my piece of pork.

ELAINE: But I want you to have your piece of pork.

DONALD: I am happy to forego my piece of pork, darling.

ELAINE: But I made it for you!

DONALD: I can easily just eat the vegetables.

ELAINE: But that's…

DONALD: I am not a great pork fan anyway.

ELAINE: Are you not?

DONALD: It's not my favourite meat.

ELAINE: (*Stamping her foot.*) Oh God…

(*There is now a loud sawing, metal grating on metal, coming from somewhere above.*)

DONALD: Oh God…

ELAINE: He said it wouldn't take him long.

DONALD: This is hardly going to be conducive to a relaxing family evening, is it?

ELAINE: I did think it best to get it over with now so…

(*The sawing continues.*

BEN saunters in.

The sawing continues. It suddenly stops.)

BEN: I'm really sorry about the mix-up.

DONALD: She's only prepared the four pieces of pork.

BEN: Really?

ELAINE: It doesn't matter…

BEN: Well, look, if it helps… I am happy to forego my piece of pork.

ELAINE: No…really and truly…

BEN: I'm not really a great pork fan, to be honest.

ELAINE: Are you not?

BEN: I'm happy to just have the vegetables if you…

DONALD: It's alright…

ELAINE: Have you both turned bloody Muslim all of a sudden!?

BEN: He's here by the way.

DONALD: Is he?

BEN: Just arrived.

DONALD: Excellent.

(*The sawing starts up again. They stand in silence as it continues. It then stops.*)

ELAINE: And I've only done the four portions of dessert.

DONALD: Look, it really doesn't matter, does it?

BEN: I'm really sorry about this.

(*Then CATRIONA walks into the room holding hands with TOM. He is roughly the same age as DONALD, though he is a trendy, leather jacket-wearing geezer. He walks with a slight limp.*

A long silence. DONALD is stunned. The silence builds. It is excruciating.

Eventually ELAINE shakes herself out of her shock and greets them.)

ELAINE: I'm really pleased to… we're really pleased to meet you. Both of you. You both. Yes. Sorry. We are. Pleased. Yes. Welcome. Welcome.

TOM: Nice to meet you.

(*No response.*)

Thanks very much for inviting me.

(*He steps forward to shake hands with DONALD.*

DONALD does not move.

A long silence. Then the sound of loud hammering.

They all stare at their feet. The hammering continues.)

End of Act One.

Act Two

SCENE 1

The living room.

DONALD, ELAINE, BEN and CATRIONA are standing in the room with their drinks. Both DONALD and BEN are now pretty drunk. DONALD is silently seething. Nobody speaks for some time until:

ELAINE: I just wanted to encapsulate the best of English design all through the ages. All through the house.

BEN: Amazing.

  (A very long silence.)

  And the pork was…amazing.

ELAINE: I think it might have been a tad overdone.

  (A long silence.)

  Do you like the coffee table?

BEN: It's…amazing.

ELAINE: The previous owners had left this hideous 1970s thing that I've somehow managed to convert with these scaffolding planks here.

BEN: Amazing.

ELAINE: I then stained it with wax and screwed these studs into the top.

  (A long silence.)

  (To CATRIONA.) Do you know Rolls and Rems at all?

CATRIONA: *(After a pause.)* Sorry, no.

  (A long silence.)

BEN: Clever, isn't she?

ELAINE: It's something I've always been interested in actually. I mean, I would have liked to…

DONALD: Very.

  (A long silence.)

ELAINE: I made the fire surround from a railway sleeper. Found it on one of my walks.

  (A long silence.)

BEN: So…Dad…what say we check these fireworks out. Up on the roof?

(*No response from DONALD.*)
Always loved Bonfire Nights. Ever since I was a kid.
Raking up the leaves and stuffing them into the Guy. That
man from next door used to make treacle toffee you could
crack your jaw on.
(*A long silence.*)
Apparently you can see every display in London from up
there.
(*No-one responds.*)
Everything alright, Dad?
(*No response.*)
Great wine.
(*No response.*)
(*Pompous voice, hoping to amuse with a well-worn family
joke.*) The Bordeaux I found had strong blackcurrant and
cedarwood aromas followed by crisp acidity, with
deliciously rich redcurrant fruit and firm tannins.
(*No response.*)
Whereas this 1998 Chianti is evocative of deep, black fruit.
A huge wash of cherries and the flavour of a black-forest
gateau.
(*No response.*)
One felt that the grape had been lovingly…
DONALD: For Christ's sake, Ben…
(*A long, awkward silence.*)
ELAINE: Do you want to take Ben and Catriona up to see the
    fireworks, darling?
DONALD: If that's what they want.
    (*A long silence.*)
ELAINE: So…shall we…?
    (*Nobody moves. A long silence.*)
    Right. Okay. Well… I think I might go and wash up…
DONALD: Forget the washing up.
ELAINE: Well…
DONALD: Lidija will do it in the morning.
ELAINE: I know but…
DONALD: That's what we pay her for, isn't it?
ELAINE: I know but, as I've said, she's not terribly good.

DONALD: Well, sack her then.

ELAINE: I don't like to.

DONALD: Get someone else in.

ELAINE: (*A slight laugh.*) It's not really my forté…hiring and firing.

BEN: And what I always say is…dishwashers don't just stack themselves, do they?
(*He laughs. The laugh peters out. A long silence.*)

DONALD: Do it in the morning, please.

ELAINE: Fine.
(*A long silence.*)
So…maybe Catriona, you'd like to see the rest of the…

DONALD: (*Suddenly, furiously.*) The man is twice your age, for Christ's sake!! What in God's name are you thinking of?!!
(*A long, embarrassed silence.*
ELAINE coughs.
The silence builds until:)

BEN: So when did you say the baby was due?

ELAINE: Next month.

BEN: That's amazing.
(*A silence.*)
You after a boy or a girl?

ELAINE: We don't mind.

BEN: Just as long as it's healthy?

ELAINE: That's right.

BEN: My little brother.

ELAINE: Yes.

BEN: Or sister.

ELAINE: (*After a pause.*) That's right.

BEN: Half.

ELAINE: (*After a pause.*) Yes.
(*A long silence. It builds.*)

CATRIONA: Actually, come to think of it, I think we'd better be off.

ELAINE: Really?

BEN: You don't want to see the fireworks then?

DONALD: Could I have a word?

CATRIONA: I'm sorry?

DONALD: A word. You and me. Could we?

CATRIONA: What about?

ELAINE: Look, I'm going to get the coffee. Right. I'll leave you three to… Okay.

(*ELAINE leaves.*

DONALD, CATRIONA and BEN are left.

The silence grows.)

BEN: I'll tell you what, Dad, this vino is bloody…

DONALD: Listen, I'll come straight to the point, Catriona. I'm… (*He breaks off.*) This man… Are you serious or…? I mean, is this a serious thing you've got going on or…?

CATRIONA: Am I serious?

DONALD: Yes?

CATRIONA: You know me.

DONALD: You are serious?

CATRIONA: I am always serious.

DONALD: But are you serious about…?

CATRIONA: Always. Serious. Me.

DONALD: I can't say, Catriona, that I'm altogether happy about this.

(*No response.*)

What about your mother? What does she have to say?

(*No response.*)

You know, we've been so worried about you. For such a long time. You go out there, where you've no business going, on some foolhardy mission to save the world, to the most dangerous place on the planet, having renounced your extremely expensive education and you… oh, I don't know. And now you come home with some…some limping man in tow, whose old enough to be your…

(*No response.*)

Is he married?

(*DONALD takes a big slug of scotch.*)

BEN: He seems like quite a nice bloke to me, Dad.

DONALD: I beg your pardon?

BEN: I said he seems like a nice enough…

DONALD: Does he indeed?

BEN: Kind of admire someone who…

DONALD: And do you…love him?

CATRIONA: He's a very brave man who…

DONALD: For Christ's sake, girl, at your age you don't have the first idea what love is!!

(*A long silence.*
TOM comes in.
The silence builds.)

TOM: It's a wonderful old house you have. Mid-Victorian at a guess?

BEN: You said 1859, Dad, didn't you?

TOM: Height of the Empire?

BEN: Absolutely. A good year.

TOM: That was the year, I think, that Darwin published *The Origin of Species.*

BEN: Course, yes.

TOM: The first nail in the coffin of organised religion.

BEN: About time too!

DONALD: (*Sullen.*) The theory of evolution is simply a theory. It describes only a process. It cannot possibly explain the first act of creation.

TOM: Well, that's a…

DONALD: It does not, and never will, explain away the existence of God.

(*A long silence.*)

TOM: Wasn't 1859 also the year of the Indian Army mutiny?

BEN: Lets bring in the expert here, shall we? Father?

DONALD: I really don't know.

TOM: The Muslims objected to having to grease their rifle cartridges with pig fat.

BEN: (*Laughing.*) That does sound pretty disgusting.

(*The laugh peters out.*
People stare at their feet.)

(*To DONALD.*) You said that the man who built the house had trading links with India, didn't you, Dad? Something to do with tea?

(*No response.*)

TOM: Anyway…it was a lovely meal.

BEN: Wasn't it just?

TOM: Really…good.

(*DONALD suddenly storms out of the room.*
A long silence.)

CATRIONA: Sorry.

TOM: Maybe it was to be expected.

BEN: Maybe.

(*CATRIONA and TOM look at BEN.*)

CATRIONA: We'd better just go.

BEN: But you've only just got here.

TOM: Your sister *has* been through a lot, Ben…

CATRIONA: I'm perfectly alright.

BEN: She's quite a tough old cookie, you know.

TOM: Of course. Yes.

CATRIONA: I'm just not really enjoying my father's company.

BEN: He's had a tough time as well, you know.

CATRIONA: Has he?

BEN: With Mum and Elaine and then all the press and the house and then what happened in September and…?

CATRIONA: How has that been tough for Dad?

BEN: I just meant…this campaign and…

TOM: Come on, Cat…

BEN: I just think he has his doubts about…

TOM: Come on. Lets not…

CATRIONA: People always talk such ill-informed…

TOM: Yes. Yes, they do.

(*A long silence.*
BEN knocks back his glass of wine. Pours another from the bottle in his hand.)

So…it was good to see you again, Ben.

BEN: Good to see you.

TOM: Hopefully we'll meet again.

BEN: Hopefully.

TOM: Some sunny day.

(*Now voices can be heard from the next room.*)

ELAINE: (*Off.*) So what do you expect me to do, just throw him out?

DONALD: (*Off.*) I didn't say that!

ELAINE: (*Off.*) You need to be a little more civil…

DONALD: (*Off.*) Alright, alright!

ELAINE: (*Off.*) And will you try not to shout, please? They're only in the next room.

DONALD: (*Off.*) What on earth is she thinking of?

ELAINE: (*Off.*) So while they are in our house they are still our guests, Donald.

DONALD: (*Off.*) No coffee for me, thank you!

ELAINE: (*Off.*) And so we must at least try to be civilised, mustn't we…

DONALD: (*Off.*) Elaine, please…

ELAINE: (*Off.*) What?

DONALD: (*Off.*) I don't want a fucking lecture, thank you. Do you understand? Now is neither the time nor the…

ELAINE: (*Off.*) Just keep your voice down.

DONALD: (*Off.*) Did you see the way he was looking at her all through dinner? He's infatuated.

ELAINE: (*Off.*) Lets just…

DONALD: (*Off.*) Practically ravishing her with his eyes!

ELAINE: (*Off.*) He seems like a genuine…

DONALD: (*Off.*) To throw her life away on a loser like that…

ELAINE: (*Off.*) He seems quite charming.

DONALD: (*Off.*) I just cannot believe it. I thought we'd brought her up to be at least a little bit more selective…

ELAINE: (*Off.*) Well, I think that…

DONALD: (*Off.*) Are you going to let me get a fucking word in edgeways, Elaine!?

(*A long silence.*

CATRIONA, TOM and BEN are staring at their feet.)

ELAINE: (*Off.*) You promised me you would try to watch your language.

DONALD: (*Off.*) Yes.

ELAINE: (*Off.*) And you're drinking far too…

DONALD: (*Off.*) Oh balls…

ELAINE: (*Off.*) You're drinking it like it's Ribena.

DONALD: (*Off.*) Yes.

ELAINE: (*Off.*) It's poison, Donald.

DONALD: (*Off.*) Yes, yes…

ELAINE: (*Off.*) And you change when you drink.

DONALD: (*Off.*) I don't.

ELAINE: (*Off.*) I'm not altogether sure I like you when you drink.

DONALD: (*Off.*) Lets just…

ELAINE: (*Off.*) Listen…the only reason I'm going on about this so much, and I'm really sorry that it's evidently driving you round the bend, is that I happen to be carrying your child. And when a woman is in this condition it is quite nice for her to have someone around who is capable of acting carefully and soberly in the event of an emergency. Someone upon whom she can…

DONALD: (*Off.*) She is a massively intelligent young woman and look at her. She drops out of Cambridge before she's about to take her finals, she buggers off to a warzone, she nearly gets herself killed in the process and now she's shacking up with some ageing…

ELAINE: (*Off.*) You don't know that they're actually…

DONALD: (*Off.*) Come on, why wouldn't he? She's a beautiful, bright young woman. Look at her. And look at him. I just can't believe it. Mary will be absolutely devastated.

ELAINE: (*Off.*) You don't know that…

DONALD: (*Off.*) I really need to see her. My wife. I have to see her.

ELAINE: (*Off.*) You also promised me you'd stop referring to her as your wife…

DONALD: (*Off.*) I really feel the need.

ELAINE: (*Off.*) She's your ex-wife, Donald. The divorce…

DONALD: (*Off.*) I miss her, you know.

ELAINE: (*Off.*) She'll probably just be glad that her daughter's come home alive and well and…

DONALD: (*Off.*) I'm so bloody angry, Elaine, I can't tell you…

(*A door slams somewhere off.*)

ELAINE: (*Off, to herself.*) You bloody…man!!

(*A very long silence in the living room.*)

BEN: Really good wine this.

TOM: You do seem to be enjoying it.

BEN: Bloody good. Amazing.

(*A long silence.*)

TOM: You a wine expert?

BEN: So…how long have you two been an item then?

(*We now hear voices off again.*)

ELAINE: (*Off.*) And nobody seemed to like my pork.

DONALD: (*Off.*) This is so unlike her!

ELAINE: (*Off.*) Did you hear?

DONALD: (*Off.*) What, what, what?!!

ELAINE: (*Off.*) Stop talking to me like that, please?

DONALD: (*Off.*) Like what?

ELAINE: (*Off.*) I said that nobody liked my pork.

DONALD: (*Off.*) I'm not interested in the fucking pork.

ELAINE: (*Off.*) And will you please keep your voice down?

DONALD: (*Off.*) He just sat there with that sheepish little smirk on his face.

ELAINE: (*Off.*) She was pushing it around her plate like it was the most revolting…

DONALD: (*Off.*) Elaine, nobody cares about the fucking pork!

ELAINE: (*Off.*) Did you like yours? You didn't, did you?

DONALD: (*Off.*) I did, I did, I did. I told you over dinner.

ELAINE: (*Off.*) What was wrong with it?

DONALD: (*Off.*) Oh, it was fine.

ELAINE: (*Off.*) If it was a little bit crisp then it was hardly my fault, was it?

DONALD: (*Off.*) Look, it doesn't matter.

ELAINE: (*Off.*) So embarrassing.

DONALD: (*Off.*) Forget it, please!!!

ELAINE: (*Off.*) Go to all that effort and people are just so…

(*A very long silence in the living room.*

BEN coughs. He then smiles awkwardly at TOM. Shrugs.)

BEN: Bit pissed actually.

TOM: (*Polite laugh.*) Right…

ELAINE: (*Off.*) Will you just take this in and please be a little bit more civil towards our guests?

BEN: (*To TOM.*) I notice you're not partaking.

TOM: No.

BEN: (*Slight laugh.*) Why's that…bad hangover or…?

TOM: I'm an alcoholic.

(*DONALD comes in, carrying a tray of coffee and cups.*

A long silence.)

BEN: Shall I help you with that, Dad?

DONALD: Thanks.

(*BEN takes the tray and sets it on the coffee table. They all watch him in silence.*)

BEN: Shall I play Mother then?

DONALD: Not ready yet.

BEN: No. Have to wait for the…push the thing down and then… Sorry.

(*Nobody speaks. The silence builds. It is excruciating.*

A loud firework close by.

CATRIONA flinches.

Again, nobody speaks. After a long time:)

DONALD: (*With forced jollity.*) Look, it would be great if you could all stay a bit longer and watch the firework show from the roof. We'd like that. If you could. Sort of…break the house in. We've not really had time for a…house-warming as yet so… So, Cat. Would you…?

(*No response.*)

Ben?

BEN: I'm always up for a party, Dad.

DONALD: And you?

TOM: I think I'd better get Catriona to…

CATRIONA: I really don't care. Don't care at all.

(*A long silence.*)

DONALD: Right. Good. That's settled then.

(*A very long silence.*)

(*Slapping his hands together, cordially.*) So…Tom…tell me: what was it that prompted you to go and work in the Middle East?

TOM: It's a long story.

DONALD: I'm all ears.

(*TOM and CATRIONA exchange a look.*)

TOM: Eight years ago I was involved in a serious car accident. I was in a coma for over a month. And while I was in this coma I had what can only be described as an out-of-body experience that lasted or seemed to last for the whole period I was unconscious. And in this extended dream,

if you like, I was herding cattle in a desert. In Palestine.
It was the most bizarre thing. It's very hard to describe.
Hour by hour, day by day, week by week I was there,
living among these people. A totally different person. And
when I finally came out of this dream, I somehow knew, I
knew in my bones, that my old life was over. I felt, having
survived the accident, that I was already dead somehow
and I had this compulsion to go and do something for
humanity. I'd never done anything to benefit other people
before. And you know how it is, Donald, when you get to
our age and you have a kind of life crisis and… Anyway
I wanted to turn my back on creature comforts and get
out there. Get my hands dirty. Open myself up to life a
little, get out of the office and the routine and the constant
work and this bloody lifestyle we all lead which had made
me so miserable and which had contributed to what had
happened to me.
(*A long silence.*)

DONALD: And before that you were…?

TOM: An architect. Designing endless McDonald's restaurants.
(*Silence in the room. Then another firework.*)
I used to drink. I was very drunk. When I crashed the car.
(*A long silence.*)
And so when I came out of hospital I resigned my
position and gave my life to helping out displaced farmers.
(*A pause.*) Land reclamation. Irrigation.
(*A long silence.*
They all watch BEN as he starts to pour the coffee drunkenly.
Nobody speaks. The silence builds.*)

BEN: How do you have it?

TOM: Just black, please.

BEN: Just black.
(*He pours the coffee. Nobody speaks. He passes a cup to TOM.*)

TOM: Thanks.

BEN: Just black.
(*A long silence.*)
Dad?

DONALD: No.

BEN: Cat?

CATRIONA: No thanks.

> (*BEN pours her coffee.*
> *They all watch him in silence.*
> *He hands it to her.*)

CATRIONA: No thanks, I said.

BEN: Course. Sorry. No thanks. No.

> (*He puts the cup back on the tray.*
> *A long silence.*
> *ELAINE comes on.*)

ELAINE: (*Cheerful.*) So…how are we all doing in here then?

BEN: Fine.

ELAINE: That's good then.

BEN: (*To ELAINE.*) How do you take your…

ELAINE: (*To DONALD.*) Do you have this money, Donald?

BEN: (*Trailing off.*) …coffee?

ELAINE: Mitch says he's almost done. And he's rather…eager to be paid.

DONALD: How much?

ELAINE: A thousand for the wall and five hundred for the plumbing.

DONALD: He's only been up there for an hour!

ELAINE: Yes but I think he has managed to fix…

DONALD: I don't know anyone who earns five hundred pounds an hour.

CATRIONA: You surprise me.

DONALD: I beg your pardon?

ELAINE: I think we'd better just pay him, darling. He seems to be a little…

DONALD: I haven't got that amount on me. Can't he come back on Monday?

BEN: I'll go for you, Dad.

DONALD: Will you?

CATRIONA: We'll all go.

BEN: It's okay.

CATRIONA: I could do with a walk.

BEN: It's not a problem.

CATRIONA: Why don't the three of us go?

ELAINE: I was going to show you round the rest of the house, wasn't I?

CATRIONA: (*After a pause.*) Yes.

ELAINE: (*A slight laugh.*) I'd really value your opinion on my modest home improvements.

CATRIONA: Fine.

BEN: How much should I...?

ELAINE: Fifteen hundred.

DONALD: Wait a minute.

ELAINE: That's what he...

DONALD: I am not paying him five hundred pounds for...

ELAINE: Alright, alright... Whatever you say.

BEN: Could I maybe have your card then?

> (*DONALD is somewhere else, soothing painful temples with his fingers.*
> *Suddenly very loud drilling starts up somewhere above. It continues.*
> *They all slowly stare up at the ceiling.*)

SCENE 2

The garden.

CATRIONA on the swing alone. She begins to sob gently. The occasional firework illuminates the scene. After a time TOM comes out from the house. He looks up at the sky as another firework explodes overhead.

TOM: So...what do you want to do?

CATRIONA: I don't know.

TOM: You want to go?

CATRIONA: I don't know.

TOM: Perhaps you'll just have to put your differences of opinion aside.

> (*A long silence.*
> *A firework.*)

CATRIONA: We used to go on marches. Seemed like every weekend. Him and Mum were great organisers. It was great fun. Red rosettes. Meetings in pubs. They had all these wonderful friends. It was all so...hopeful, so idealistic. And I felt a part of it. Even as a child. To see him then you would not believe it. He was fresh-faced, big smile, long-hair, scruffy denims, chanting JOBS NOT BOMBS at the top of his voice.

TOM: More than I ever did.

CATRIONA: And the way Mum used to look at him when he gave his speeches. With such love, with such…admiration. They were both such heroes to me. I mean, these were busy people. She was a doctor, he was a lawyer but they always had time to leaflet people and campaign and demonstrate and get drunk with their mates and bring us up and what they used to talk about made so much sense. And they were all so passionate, so angry. And Mum and Dad seemed to have this perfect, equal, supportive relationship. They would argue about politics and books and music and they'd always be kissing each other and they just seemed like these gods to me. He seemed like a…Superman. (*A pause.*) Mum's kept the faith of course but he just seems so…alone.

TOM: Well, we're all alone, aren't we?
(*A long silence.*
A firework.)
I've been helping Elaine load her brand new dishwasher.

CATRIONA: Good for you.

TOM: She seems like a…nice woman.

CATRIONA: Slightly more worshipping than my mother.

TOM: I imagine so.

CATRIONA: Though I doubt she'll be as broad-minded about his affairs.
(*A loud firework explodes overhead. It startles her slightly.*
A silence.)
I don't know what to say to him. It's like he can't look me in the eye any more. It's like I've lost him.
(*He begins slowly to push her on the swing.*)
I'm sick of living in this world, Tom. This rotten, stinking, murdering world.

TOM: I know.

CATRIONA: I need to talk to someone.

TOM: Talk to me.

CATRIONA: Someone…objective.

(*Another firework.*)

And anyway it seems so self-indulgent, so pathetic to feel like this. When I can leave there any time I want. I can come back to…all of this. Any time I want. A career. Money. Comfort.

TOM: And do you want to?

CATRIONA: If I belong anywhere I belong over there.

I feel…almost functional.

(*Another firework.*)

TOM: It'll kill you. You can't save the world on your own. You're too young. You're too smart. You've got too much to offer.

CATRIONA: They have to have their land back. They simply have to have their land back and then…and then maybe all this will…

(*Another firework.*)

TOM: Cat, listen, I want to come home. I don't want to share a shack with eight people any more. Living like a student. I want to come home now.

(*Another firework.*)

But I want to come home with you. I feel like I've been of some use out there. I've helped build some decent things and made a few people's lives a bit less unpleasant. I've enjoyed it but… I'm English. And I want to die in England.

CATRIONA: You're not that old.

TOM: I miss the place. There's a lot about England I miss.

CATRIONA: I didn't know that.

TOM: Sitting in a pub on a Sunday afternoon with the paper. The cold weather. Novembers. Decembers. When it's dark at four, when the leaves go red. I miss my friends. Football.

CATRIONA: So you're finishing then?

TOM: It depends.

CATRIONA: And what will you do…go back to McDonald's?

TOM: Who knows?

CATRIONA: But they rely on people like you. With your skills. You really want to come back to this…this broken country?

TOM: It's my home.
(*A long silence.*)
And Catriona…I'm deeply, deeply in love with you. You know that. (*A long pause.*) Will you marry me?
(*CATRIONA stops the swing. She rises. She walks away. She does not speak.*)
Marriage has never been my thing, I know, but since I've met you I…
(*No response.*)
I'm ready for it now. Children later. If you like. I want to settle. I could get another job or even go back to the firm, I'm sure they'd have me despite… And I've got some money saved up. From the sale of the house. We could get a little place. Get away from all the death, all the violence. All that pain. It's hard to live amongst all the hate. You said so yourself. We could lead an ordinary life. You could go back to Cambridge, get on with a career, maybe even dance again or whatever you…
(*No response. She looks out front.*)
And I've never said that to anyone else before. Never felt it. But it feels right now. Like it all makes a bit of sense at last. I always thought I was destined to die alone. Some grizzled old bachelor who thinks he's lived a life but hasn't really lived at all. And look, we don't have to get married but…if that's what you want, then… All I mean is…I'd like to make an honest woman of you. A commitment.
(*Another firework.*)
And now that I'm off the booze and it's all behind me, I feel I can finally face the future with a bit of…optimism.
CATRIONA: Optimism?
TOM: Optimism. Yes. Why not?
(*Another firework.*)
I just think we both deserve a little happiness now. (*He breaks off. A long silence.*) Say something.
CATRIONA: I'm twenty-five years old.
(*He approaches her slowly. He puts a hand on her shoulder.*)

Maybe tonight's not the best time to spring this on you but…I don't know…just looking at you in there… the way you deal with your dreadful family and…

CATRIONA: What do you mean, dreadful?

TOM: Well…all families are dreadful, aren't they? I thought we'd already established that?

(*Another firework.*)

You're not going to spend the rest of your life in a refugee camp, surely? You said you wanted kids one day. Well…so do I. I think we'd be great parents and…what more can I say? I'm offering you my life. I can't let you go. Really. If I can't have you then…

(*Another firework.*)

You're making me nervous. You're making me…

CATRIONA: (*Through tears.*) You've lost your balls, Tom.

TOM: No.

CATRIONA: You crave the western bourgeois life after all.

TOM: I'm just sick of being…

CATRIONA: I'm sorry but…we have to end this.

(*Another firework.*

A long silence.)

TOM: What?

CATRIONA: We have to. I'm sorry.

TOM: What are you talking about?

CATRIONA: It's just not right any more.

(*A long silence.*)

TOM: I can't believe you're saying this. You want us to finish?

CATRIONA: Yes.

TOM: Okay, well, look…we don't need to get married. I mean, I didn't want to scare you off but…for Christ's sake… you're breaking my heart here, you're…

CATRIONA: I'm sorry.

TOM: So you keep saying.

CATRIONA: I don't want to be with you.

TOM: (*Devastated.*) Cat…

CATRIONA: It's finished.

TOM: You're saying you don't love me? Are you? After what we've been through? That what you're saying? You are

what I get out of bed for. You take that away from me
then…
(*Another firework.*)
Are you telling me you don't love me?
(*Another firework.*)
Then why the hell did you bring me here? Just to get back
at him!?
(*Another firework.*)
(*Exploding, grabbing her arm.*) Will you please fucking talk to
me!!!

CATRIONA: What kind of person has children anyway?
Bringing innocent human beings into all of this?
(*A long silence.*)

TOM: My whole life is just…my whole life is falling apart
again.
(*BEN drunkenly saunters on, bottle of wine in one hand, glass
in the other.*)

BEN: Alright, folks?
(*No response.*)
Something of an atmosphere in there.
(*No response.*)
I would venture that they might be having some form of
crisis actually.
(*No response.*)
Also: seems Father has something of a cash-flow problem.
(*No response.*)
Could not extract a single coin from his current account.
(*No response.*)
Checked his balance actually.
(*No response.*)
Bit naughty, I know but…
(*No response.*)
Talk about an overdraft.
(*No response.*)
Bit pissed actually.
(*TOM leaves the garden.
CATRIONA turns and walks slowly towards BEN. As she
approaches he opens his arms slightly, still with bottle in one*

*hand and glass in the other. She walks into his arms and then
holds him, her head on his chest.
Nonplussed, he closes his arms awkwardly around her.
Fireworks.)*

SCENE 3

The living room.

DONALD, very drunk, and ELAINE. Neither speak for some time.

DONALD: I'm sorry.

ELAINE: Forget it.

DONALD: She's my daughter. I'm just a little…

ELAINE: Of course you are.

DONALD: I've made a fool of myself. I'll apologise to them.

ELAINE: They'll understand.

DONALD: You know a hospital was hit the other night?
Hundreds dead. Quite a few children. Quite a few women.

ELAINE: Donald…

DONALD: Several pregnant.

ELAINE: Do we have to talk about this now?
(*A loud firework.*)
And you didn't mean to hit it, did you?

DONALD: (*After a pause.*) No.

ELAINE: It was not your intention?

DONALD: No but…

ELAINE: There you are then.

DONALD: (*In a professional tone, though drunk.*) "It is a sad
yet inevitable fact of war that on occasions there will
be civilian casualties but you can rest assured that we
are doing everything in our power to keep these to a
minimum. But I ask you all to hold onto that feeling you
had when you saw those planes flying into those towers,
the sense of outrage, the sense of anger, the sense of
disgust. I ask you to imagine how those innocent people
felt in their last few moments on this earth. To fight this evil
we must remain resolute. Terrorism will not be defeated
by pacifism and blind optimism. This is the modern world
and this is a modern war."

(*He takes a large slug of alcohol.*)

ELAINE: Donald, you are drinking far too much.

DONALD: Yes.

ELAINE: So, please will you…

DONALD: *They* know it's about oil, *we* know it's about oil.

(*A loud firework.*)

The whole world knows it's about fucking oil.

ELAINE: It's about protecting civilisation.

DONALD: Ah. I was forgetting.

ELAINE: And freedom, Donald.

DONALD: Oh, don't talk to me about fucking freedom!

ELAINE: Okay, I'm leaving you to it if you're going to be like
this…

(*DONALD holds her by the arm.*)

DONALD: (*Staring drunkenly into her face.*) Oh Christ, what have
I done?

ELAINE: What do you mean by that?

DONALD: Nothing.

ELAINE: I'm not quite sure how to take that.

(*A loud firework*
A long silence.)

Donald…are you happy with me?

DONALD: (*After a pause.*) Course.

ELAINE: Why do you say it like that?

DONALD: I'm tired. Please. Not tonight.

ELAINE: You would have the courage though, wouldn't you?
To tell me?

DONALD: Tell you what?

ELAINE: If you ever stopped…loving me?

DONALD: Elaine, lets not…tonight…lets not…

ELAINE: Nothing I say interests you, does it? Not really?
I never make you laugh, do I? Not like Mary did.

(*No response.*)

You are so drunk.

DONALD: I know.

ELAINE: So, so drunk.

DONALD: Yes.

ELAINE: I just don't know why you always insist on…

DONALD: (*Exploding.*) Elaine, please, will you just stop fucking whining at me for one single second, PLEASE!!!
(*IAN enters. A tense, silence.*)

IAN: (*Jovially.*) Any chance of a brew then?

ELAINE: I beg your pardon?

IAN: All done up there.

ELAINE: Thank you.

IAN: Or maybe I could just have one of what he's having?

ELAINE: ⎱⎰ Of course.

DONALD: ⎰⎱ I'm sorry but this is neither the…
(*She snatches DONALD's glass from his hand and passes it to IAN.*)

IAN: Most kind.
(*A long silence. He drinks.*)
So…you got me money then, sunshine?

DONALD: I beg your pardon?

IAN: Me fifteen hundred quid?

DONALD: We're having something of a problem here actually and so I would be extremely grateful if you could…

IAN: You hear what I said?

DONALD: Listen…

IAN: (*Looking round the room.*) Yeah. It's a nice enough room, innit? (*To ELAINE.*) You done alright for yerself, haven't ya?

ELAINE: I'm not entirely sure how to take…

IAN: (*Making 'money gesture'.*) You know how to play the game alright, don't ya?

ELAINE: I'm sorry?

IAN: (*Winking at him.*) Oh yeah, she knows how to play the game alright.
(*A long silence.*)
So…? My money?

DONALD: As you can probably deduce for yourself we are entertaining this evening and so I would appreciate it greatly if you could come back on Monday morning…

IAN: I want it now.

DONALD: If you could just let me finish…

IAN: I said, I want it now.

DONALD: And I'm afraid that I am unable to oblige you at the present time since I…

IAN: Don't fuck with me.

(*A long silence.*)

DONALD: Are you threatening me?

IAN: Of course.

DONALD: Would you mind waiting outside, please!

IAN: You what?

DONALD: I said would you mind waiting outside for a moment please?

IAN: I want my money.

DONALD: Would you kindly wait outside, please?

(*A long silence. A stand-off.*)

ELAINE: Listen, Mitch, we've got a bit of a…family situation going on at the moment and as you can see from my condition…

IAN: (*Eyes fixed on DONALD.*) I want my money.

ELAINE: …and while we appreciate your hard work and your patience this evening…

IAN: Is that clear?

ELAINE: And you have been very patient with us…

IAN: I'm not leaving here…

ELAINE: Well, extremely patient…

IAN: …without it.

(*A very long silence.*)

ELAINE: (*To DONALD.*) Oh, for goodness sake, why don't you just pay him?

IAN: Wise words.

DONALD: Listen…my son has just been to the bank for me and unfortunately I'm at the limit of my overdraft facility. And so if you could come back on Monday…

IAN: Give me the money.

DONALD: ….as I say, I would be happy to oblige.

IAN: Do you understand what I'm saying to you?

(*A long silence. DONALD jangles his car keys.*)

ELAINE: Donald, you are NOT driving!

DONALD: No. Sorry. No.

(*DONALD makes a move to the exit.*)

IAN sits in the large armchair chair. He sips his scotch.
A shell-shocked TOM enters.)

TOM: Came to say goodbye.

ELAINE: But I was going to give you a guided tour, wasn't I?

TOM: Thanks for your…hospitality.

ELAINE: I was going to show you round the house? My
different designs?

TOM: Well…

ELAINE: Look, I insist. Now, please…

(She escorts the stunned man away. A silence.)

IAN: *(To DONALD.)* You got ten minutes.

(DONALD leaves.

Left alone, IAN relaxes into the chair. He then takes out his
knife. Holds it up and examines it. Thinks. He puts it back in
his jacket. He slowly rises from the chair. He walks around the
room as if he owns it. He approaches the mantelpiece. Picks up
an ornament. Then another. Pockets one.
Distant fireworks.)

SCENE 4

The roof terrace.

BEN faces front, drunker, still holding his glass and bottle. CATRIONA
sits by the back railing, her face in her hands. The fireworks seem closer
and louder as they explode throughout the scene.

BEN: *(Pacing, histrionic, drunk.)* The matter that is now to be
offered to you my Lords the Commissioners, and to the
Trial of you the Knights and Gentlemen of the Jury, is the
Matter of Treason; but of such Horror, and monstrous
Nature, that before now,
The Tongue of Man never delivered,
The Ear of Man never heard,
The Heart of Man never conceited,
Nor the Malice of hellish or earthly Devil ever practised.
For, if it be abominable to murder the least;
If to touch God's Anointed be to oppose themselves
against God;
If (by Blood) to subvert Princes, States and Kingdoms,

be hateful to God and Man, as all true Christians must
acknowledge:
Then, how much more than too too monstrous shall all
Christian Hearts judge the Horror of this Treason; to
murder and subvert
Such a King,
Such a Queen,
Such a Prince,
Such a Progeny,
Such a State,
Such a Government,
So complete and absolute,
That God approves,
The World admires,
All true English Hearts honour and reverence,
The Pope and his Disciples only envies and maligns?!!
(*A long silence.*)
See? I still remember it. The trial of one Guido Fawkes.
(*TOM comes on. He approaches CATRIONA. Stops.*)
(*Oblivious.*) Imagine being dragged through the streets,
being hanged until you're almost dead, having your nob
cut off and stuffed into your mouth, having your guts
ripped out and burned in front of you, being chopped into
quarters and then having your head stuck on a spike.
TOM: (*Quiet.*) We need to talk.
BEN: Not nice.
TOM: Cat?
BEN: Not nice by any stretch of the imagination. (*He turns and
notices TOM.*) Alright?
TOM: Cat?
BEN: Just been doing my seventeenth-century lawyer bit. Sir
Edward Philip.
TOM: Cat?
BEN: James the First's Sergeant of Law.
TOM: Please, Cat.
BEN: In the year or our Lord sixteen hundred and six.
CATRIONA: Just go. Please.
(*A loud firework. A long silence.*)

BEN: Amazing view, isn't it? Would you not say?

TOM: Listen, Ben…

BEN: So…whereabouts are you staying?

TOM: Bethnal Green.

BEN: One of our secretaries is from that neck of the woods actually.

TOM: Right.

BEN: A real 'Eastender'.

TOM: Have you been crying?

BEN: Salt of the earth.

TOM: Cat?

BEN: Nice smile actually.

TOM: Have you?

BEN: And she works terribly hard.

TOM: Please…

BEN: I expect the whole place would collapse without her actually.

TOM: Lets go.

BEN: Melanie.

TOM: (*With his hand on her shoulder.*) You need to rest.

CATRIONA: (*Shrugging him off.*) I'm alright!

BEN: Are you alright?

TOM: (*Approaching him.*) Actually, Ben, do you think you could leave us for a moment? I think Cat's a bit…

BEN: Cat?

TOM: I need to get her home.

BEN: Course.

TOM: That okay?

(*BEN moves towards the firedoor.*)

BEN: See you then.

CATRIONA: Bye.

BEN: (*To TOM.*) See you.

TOM: Thanks.

(*He staggers off.*)

CATRIONA: What is it with men and alcohol?

(*A long silence.*

A firework overhead.)

Just go.

TOM: I don't know what's happened. I thought we were going to be leaving here tonight…happy. Hopeful.

CATRIONA: It's finished. It's all finished.

(*A silence.*)

TOM: You never want to see me again?

CATRIONA: (*After a pause.*) No.

(*A silence.*)

TOM: Then my life's over. That's it. You were my…you were my last…

(*A long silence as they stare at each other.*
IAN comes on. He comes forward and looks out front.)

IAN: Jesus Christ! (*Pointing.*) Dome. Big Ben. BT Tower. London Eye. St Pancreas. Saint Paul's just there, in between those skyscrapers. Monument. See it all, can't you? Must feel like you own the whole city, having a view like this!

(*A series of fireworks close by.*
CATRIONA is now standing with TOM close to her. His hand moves slowly towards her. He gently moves some of her hair from face.
More fireworks.)

Remember, Remember, the Fifth of November, Gunpowder, Treason and…Plot.

(*TOM gently kisses CATRIONA's forehead. He leaves.*
During the following, CATRIONA slowly raises herself up on the back railing. She stands there, with the poise of a gymnast on a six-inch beam.)

Canary Wharf. I love tall buildings. Course that's not tall, is it? Only eight hundred feet high. Not like those towers. You know how tall them twin towers are? Were, sorry. One thousand eight hundred feet. Imagine that. I went up them once. Got a cousin over there. Went over as a kid. With me Mum and me brother. Went up to the viewing place. Great glass windows. And you're so high up you can't hardly see people walking about on the streets beneath you. And there's helicopters flying about under your feet. Amazing. I remember seeing this copter and it seemed to be coming right for us. One of them little tourist copters. Swooped right by us. (*A pause.*) Wish I could be that age again. Eight. I fucking loved being eight.

(*CATRIONA lifts a leg straight up, like a gymnast, and holds it there, with perfect control.*)

And I'm thinking...imagine being up there in that restaurant on that morning, laying your tables for breakfast or whatever they were doing, getting the grub ready for all them tourists and them stockbrokers and that and then suddenly out of nowhere you see this great fucking plane come flying straight for ya. Four hundred miles an hour. Grinning towelheads at the controls. Praying to Allah and that as they come right for ya. Jesus Christ. Can't get that thought out me head. And those fuckers who jumped sooner than burn. And that's a long way to fall. And you got a long time to think, haven't yer? A long time to think about your life that's nearly over. Tell the truth a part of me really enjoyed it all. It was like watching a bloody film, seeing those towers come down. And all those people inside. Jesus. It was like a film. The most amazing film you've ever seen in your whole life.

(*CATRIONA suddenly and gracefully drops over the back railing and is gone. Almost immediately the sound of breaking glass.*)

But I tell you...it's right what we're doing. No question. Giving those Pakis a right good twatting.

(*He turns to see he is alone. He turns back. Fireworks.*)

SCENE 5

The living room.

ELAINE and DONALD. He has just said something momentous. She is stunned. After a time:

ELAINE: You're drunk.

DONALD: (*Strangely animated.*) No.

ELAINE: You're not serious.

DONALD: It's the right thing to do. And on Monday I'm going in there and I'm going to do it. I feel completely liberated.

ELAINE: Hold on...

DONALD: It's all wrong, Elaine. The whole thing is just…
wrong.

ELAINE: But what's made you…

DONALD: I'm walking back from the bank. It's a beautiful
night, it's happy out there. It's London. The nicest part
of London, these wonderful houses, these expensive cars,
these stunning kitchens you can see into, and all these
happy people enjoying their Saturday nights, kids out
with sparklers and coats and rushing to the parks and…it's
England, it's…us. And I'm thinking…and I'm thinking…
that I've been so miserable for so long and I don't know
why and it's all this regret. I live with it all the time and it's
choking me, Elaine. And then this firework exploded just
outside the house. It was so loud that I heard a window
smashing, or glass breaking. It nearly knocked me off my
feet and then I heard this baby crying next door. It must
have scared this baby to death, these bloody explosions all
night long and then I'm thinking, I'm thinking that this is
all wrong, that this is all so wrong. I don't want to be killing
people. I don't want any part in killing people. Guilty
people or innocent people or any people.

ELAINE: But you cannot just…resign.

DONALD: I am against this. I am. Against this. I have always
been…against this.

ELAINE: No.

DONALD: I don't know who I am any more. Do you know
what that feels like? Have you any idea? I've been a man
who's always been sure of his direction. But now I'm lost.
So lost and my daughter…she's right. She's right and I
have to tell her. I…

ELAINE: You need to stop drinking.

DONALD: Yes.

ELAINE: It makes you depressed.

DONALD: I'll never drink again. I swear. This is it.

ELAINE: And you're not going to resign?

DONALD: You have to support me in this. I can no longer
participate in it. Mary is right, Catriona is right. These
people are right.

ELAINE: We'll talk tomorrow.

DONALD: I need to see my daughter. Tell her. I need her to love me again.

ELAINE: She does love you.

DONALD: And she was always so happy. They both were. My daughter, my wife and…

ELAINE: I don't want to hear this.

DONALD: We were so happy and…

ELAINE: I really don't want to hear this actually.

DONALD: Catriona with her bunches and her ballet shoes. And she was such a dancer. She was the best in her class. She had so much grace. And we'd sit there at the back and we'd be glowing with pride and she'd do these moves that were…the other parents would gasp and we'd be so proud and I have to see her. Where is she?

ELAINE: They're waiting for you on the roof.

DONALD: I'm serious, Elaine. I'm finished with it.

ELAINE: Donald, you are not serious. Believe me.

DONALD: Elaine, understand: I…do…not…believe…in…it.

ELAINE: (*Snapping.*) What do you mean you don't believe in it? What the hell do you mean, Donald? We have just bought this house! We are having a baby! This is what you wanted! I have supported you all this time! I have supported you for years, all the way through, when you left Mary, when the chips were down, I've supported you. And you wanted this house. You've worked hard, we've both worked hard. And we need the money, darling. We are in debt up to our eyeballs, Donald! So I'm afraid that we really need the money. And we really need you to continue in your job. We need every bloody penny we can get!
(*A long silence.*
A distant firework.
DONALD goes to the armchair and sits. He stares at his feet in despair.
After a time ELAINE goes to him.)
(*Kindly.*) Darling, I am here for you. I am always here for you. You know that.

DONALD: (*Looking up, serious.*) I miss my Mary. I just miss my
wife. I miss her. I really, really, really...miss her.
(*ELAINE turns and storms out of the room.*
DONALD sits alone, his head tilted right back.)

SCENE 6

The roof terrace.

*IAN alone. He drinks. Looks at his watch. The fireworks increase in
intensity throughout the scene. DONALD comes sadly on. IAN turns.
Neither speak for some time.*

DONALD: I'm afraid you're going to have to accept a cheque.

IAN: Sorry?

DONALD: I have no cash. (*A pause.*) I apologise.

IAN: You're telling me you live in a house like this, with a view
like this and that you have no cash?

DONALD: That's exactly what I'm telling you.

IAN: Give me your wallet.

DONALD: I beg your pardon?

IAN: Give me your wallet.

DONALD: I cannot access any money until next week.

IAN: I want your cards and I want your cash.

DONALD: Listen...
(*IAN takes out his knife and moves towards DONALD.*)
Listen...seriously...I don't have any money.

IAN: Give me your wallet or I'll slice you to pieces.
(*IAN now stands between DONALD and the door.*)
Just give it to me.
(*DONALD takes out his wallet and throws it to IAN.*
IAN opens it and removes the cards.)
I want your PIN numbers. Write them down.

DONALD: There is nothing in the account. In any account.

IAN: Just do it.

DONALD: I don't have a pen.

IAN: (*In desperation.*) Look, I want the money. I need the
money.

DONALD: But I don't have it...

IAN: If I don't get the money then I'm fucked. I'm fucked and if I'm fucked then you're fucked.

DONALD: Please. Next week…

IAN: Then you're going to bleed.

DONALD: Please.

IAN: You're really going to bleed.

(*IAN approaches DONALD holding the knife towards him.*)

DONALD: Please…I have a baby on the way and…

IAN: This is going to give me some serious pleasure. A nice long scar across the mouth and cheek, I think.

(*DONALD is backing away, coming dangerously close to the front of the roof.*

IAN brandishes the knife close to him.

Dodging it, DONALD slips, and he falls on his back.

IAN stands over him, menacing and triumphant over the squirming man.)

This is to teach you that you have to pay your way in this life. And you'll have a permanent reminder of our little meeting tonight.

(*He is about to attack DONALD with the knife when BEN comes charging from the door. He rugby-tackles IAN and sends him crashing to the floor. The knife goes flying from his hand and soon he has the man pinned down, holding him savagely by the throat.*)

BEN: This man here, this man lying here is my father, you understand? And I love him. Do you love your father? Do you even know who your father is? Probably not. But I do. I know who my father is. And you do not, I repeat, you do not touch him. You got that? You do not touch my father! I love him. You know what love is, do you? And nobody… and I mean nobody…touches my father. Is that clear? Especially not a little oik like you. Do you understand?

(*IAN croaks incoherently.*)

So…what do you say? I think it's about time we escorted you from the premises, isn't it?

(*IAN croaks incoherently.*)

And you can count yourself extremely fortunate that I haven't ripped both your arms from your body.

(BEN gets up, yanks IAN to his feet and frogmarches him, an arm behind his back, away.
A huge firework explodes and its colours light up the stage.)

SCENE 7

The garden.

Darkness in the garden. As the fireworks explode into life, a figure is illuminated on the swing. This we can tell is TOM. After a time he lifts up a bottle of wine. He looks at it for several seconds. Then he brings it to his mouth and takes a long swig.

SCENE 8

The roof terrace.

DONALD, BEN, ELAINE. They stand in silence, watching the displays. The fireworks are much closer and louder than before. In fact the explosions should now be shaking the auditorium. Bright, coloured lights, distant cheers.

DONALD: Where's your sister?
BEN: I don't know.
   (Behind them we now see the blue flashing lights of an ambulance and hear the siren. They are oblivious. After a time TOM comes on. They notice him. DONALD senses from him that something awful has happened.)
DONALD: Catriona?
   (TOM lowers his face and stares at his feet.
   More explosions.
   The lights now come up on the living room area:
   Water appears to be dripping down from the ceiling and is falling into the room, splashing off the cafetiere and cups on the coffee table. It starts as a gentle flow and then becomes stronger. Soon it is flowing with some force onto the coffee table. As the flashes and explosions from the fireworks continue, we become aware of a figure in the garden. He is only lit up when a firework bursts overhead. The explosions are now extremely loud, as if the house were being bombed from above.)

The figure, who is IAN, appears to be spraying a slogan across the wall and window of the house. As another flash of light illuminates him, we see that he is spraying the word THEIF (sic) across the wall in big red letters. Just as he finishes and rushes off, a huge slab of plaster drops into the living room and crashes onto the coffee table.)

Blackout and silence.

THE SWING OF THINGS

Characters

LINDSAY
mid 30s

MARK
mid 30s

RUTH
mid 30s

STEVE
40s

CLAUDE
mid 20s

CAROLINE
mid 30s

*The offstage voices of numerous
photographers*

*The play is set in Ruth's kitchen and terrace area over one
evening in early summer.*

*An exit from the kitchen leads off to the hall and front door,
and from the terrace to the garden. There are tables and chairs
in both sections and outside, leaning against the back wall,
are various garden tools: a fork, a spade, a wheelbarrow etc.
The terrace area is a complete mess and is covered with potted
plants, many of which are clearly dead.
The large branch of a tree reaches out from the garden
area (mainly unseen) and over the terrace. There is also a
wheelchair lying on its side at the back of the terrace.*

The Swing of Things was first performed on 4 October 2007 at the Stephen Joseph Theatre in Scarborough, with the following cast:

LINDSAY, Cate Hamer

MARK, Neal Barry

RUTH, Patti Clare

STEVE, Mark Spalding

CLAUDE, David Ajala

CAROLINE, Vivien Parry

Director, Adam Barnard

Designer, Nancy Surman

Lighting Designer, Julie Washington

Stage Manager, Emily Vickers

Deputy Stage Manager, Andy Hall

Assistant Stage Manager, Emma Hanson

Act One

EXORDIUM

In the terrace area. As the audience take their places, the distorted sound of teenagers playing in a swimming pool. Mocking laughter and indistinct chanting, coupled with the sound of water splashing. RUTH, who is attractive but a little overweight, is sitting at the table, head in hands. After a time she lifts her head and looks around sadly. She picks up the large glass of wine next to her and takes a slug. The sound of the laughing children in the pool increases menacingly as she does this and then slowly fades with the lights.

SCENE 1

An hour later. RUTH, drunk, is now in the kitchen slugging back another large glass of wine. On the terrace, LINDSAY and MARK are seated at the table. He is staring at the ground, she is staring at him. She is attractive but a little underweight. He is a bit of a bloke, preferably with a paunch. Neither speak for a time, until:

LINDSAY: Are you going to be like this all evening?
(*They fall back into silence.*)
Please tell me what crime I've committed.
(*No answer.*)
This is our first night out in months…the children are happy and safe and so…
(*No answer.*)
I had no idea it was going to be like this.
(*No answer.*)
(*To herself.*) Oh, for God's sake…
(*They fall back into silence.*)
It's only because we promised her one. You can't just promise the girl a horse and then turn round and tell her she can't have it. (*A pause.*) Are you absolutely sure we can't find the money from somewhere?
(*No answer.*)
And anyway, just for the record, I really don't like being called…
(*RUTH now enters the terrace with drinks for her guests.*)

…a 'stupid middle-class bitch'.
(*RUTH stops in her tracks.*
A very tense silence eventually broken by a nervous laugh from
RUTH.
RUTH puts the drinks on the table.)

RUTH: A water for you, sir.
(*No response.*)
And a wine for you, madam.
(*A long silence.*
RUTH and LINDSAY are smiling at each other.)
Doesn't the time go quickly?

LINDSAY: Certainly does.

RUTH: (*A nervous laugh.*) All soon be in our graves…
(*The laugh peters put. A tense silence.*)
You remember that party we had here?

LINDSAY: I'm not sure I…

RUTH: Fancy dress? We were thirteen or fourteen? You came
as Marilyn Monroe? (*To MARK.*) She was gorgeous.
(*A silence. They all smile politely at each other.*)

LINDSAY: Well, you've hardly changed at all.

RUTH: Oh…?

LINDSAY: What I mean is…

RUTH: I would hope that I'm a little more…

LINDSAY: Oh, of course, of course…

RUTH: A little less…

LINDSAY: Oh, absolutely. Of course. Sorry.
(*A long silence.*)

RUTH: So… Mark, what do you do again?
(*He does not respond.*)

LINDSAY: Small business.
(*A silence as RUTH waits for her to expand.*)

RUTH: Sounds…wonderful then. And so he's…a small
businessman then…?

LINDSAY: (*Patting her stomach.*) Not so small now, sadly.
(*A long silence as MARK glowers at LINDSAY.*)

RUTH: How wonderful then. (*A pause.*) And it's doing well?
(*No response.*)

LINDSAY: It's quite a success story actually and he…

MARK: Could be better.

RUTH: I see.

MARK: Could be worse.

LINDSAY: He started it from scratch.

RUTH: That's wonderful then.

LINDSAY: He employs over ten people.

MARK: Thirteen.

LINDSAY: Sorry?

MARK: I employ thirteen people.

LINDSAY: That's what I said.

MARK: You said 'over ten'.

LINDSAY: And thirteen *is* over ten, isn't it?

MARK: Then why not say 'over twelve'?

LINDSAY: Sorry.

MARK: Or, better still, 'thirteen'?

LINDSAY: (*A smile to RUTH.*) I will next time.
    (*A long silence.*)

RUTH: Well, that all sounds wonderful then.
    (*A silence.*)
    And how long have you two been together now?

MARK: } {   Too long.
LINDSAY: } {   Ten years.
    (*A long silence.*)

RUTH: Oh, that's…that's wonderful then.
    (*A long silence.*)

LINDSAY: I haven't been back here for ages.

RUTH: Well…the school is thriving. You'll be pleased to know.
    (*A silence.*)
    (*Laughing nervously.*) School. Teacher training. School. Full
    circle. Bit sad, isn't it?

LINDSAY: Not at all. If that's what you…

RUTH: Living in the same little corner I grew up in. The same
    little house.

LINDSAY: I think it's rather…

RUTH: Tragic?

LINDSAY: (*After a pause.*) No. No. Not at all. If that's what
    you…

RUTH: Not one shred of ambition, you see. (*A long pause.*)
Thank you both so much for coming.
(*A silence as they all drink.*)

LINDSAY: So…who exactly is joining us? I can't wait to see
how much everyone's…

RUTH: Caroline Denholm-Young.
(*A silence.*)

LINDSAY: Ah. You see we assumed that it was going to be a
big…

RUTH: Such a little gang, weren't we?

LINDSAY: (*After a pause.*) We were?

RUTH: Ruth, Lindsay, Caroline… always together, always
plotting something.

LINDSAY: I'm not sure I…

RUTH: You know, I had these three girls in my class who were
so like we used to be. Lucy Rogers, Emily Hamilton and
Susannah Jones. Honestly, it was the same gang. To the
letter.

LINDSAY: Really?

RUTH: It was the three of us. Carbon copies. Lucy was the
intelligent confident one, Emily the pretty but rather
insipid one and Susannah the overweight and self-hating
one.

LINDSAY: Sorry…so…which was I then?

RUTH: And that's what so strange because, Mark, until very
recently I taught in the exact same classroom that we all
used to be in. And these three girls sat at the exact same
desks that we used to.

MARK: What you teach?

RUTH: (*Laughing nervously.*) Le Français.

MARK: What, French?

RUTH: (*Nonplussed.*) Well…yes.
(*A silence.*)
Sadly I was forced to give up teaching in order to care
for my…

MARK: Don't take this the wrong way or anything…

RUTH: …to care for my…

MARK: But I can't see the point in learning French.

RUTH: ….my mother.

MARK: To be fair.

RUTH: Although, truth to tell, I suspect I jumped before I was…

MARK: The whole world speaks English now.

RUTH: …was pushed.

MARK: I suppose if you're going to bother to learn another language my advice to you would be: get your head down and learn Chinese.

(*A silence.*)

LINDSAY: And Caroline works in fashion?

MARK: 'Cos they'll be running the world in a hundred years.

LINDSAY: She was always so stylish.

MARK: I shall let you have that free of charge.

LINDSAY: I always tried to copy her but…

MARK: Did French at school. Complete waste of time.

RUTH: Yes, she's doing very well.

MARK: *Je suis, tu es, il est…*

RUTH: She did confirm she was coming but I'm still not one hundred per cent…

MARK: But if you want to run a competitive business, if you want to compete out there in the real world then, at the moment, English is the only language you're ever going to need.

RUTH: You know, bothering with us ordinary, average people.

MARK: Trust me.

RUTH: And our ordinary, average lives. (*A pause.*) She's become quite big.

LINDSAY: Oh, she's fat now, is she?

RUTH: Successful.

LINDSAY: I was going to say. She was always like a stick…

MARK: You can trust me on that.

RUTH: With these stunning supermodels gliding down catwalks in Milan and Paris and…

LINDSAY: I'd no idea she was so…

RUTH: Always knew she'd do well for herself.

MARK: It is the universal language.

LINDSAY: Well, it's not all about money, is it? Lets just hope
that she's…

MARK: End of story.

RUTH: And it all looks such fun, doesn't it?

LINDSAY: …she's happy as well.

RUTH: (*To herself.*) Such good…fun.

(*A silence.*)

You know…you could have been a model…

LINDSAY: Oh, really? I don't think I was quite…

RUTH: Well…cheers anyway. Thank you both so much for
coming.

(*A silence.*)

She's bringing a friend along. Some footballer.

LINDSAY: Oh, that'll be nice. Mark used to play a bit of…

MARK: Is he a pro?

RUTH: No. I think he's a footballer.

MARK: What?

LINDSAY: Mark wanted to be a footballer.

MARK: I *was* a footballer.

LINDSAY: Yes. Sorry. Was. One. Yes.

RUTH: How wonderful. Were you any good?

MARK: Not bad.

LINDSAY: He played for Leyton Orients actually. Played a
game for the reserves. He was…

MARK: (*Struggling with his anger.*) It's Leyton Orient! How
many times? It's Leyton Orient! Only the one Orient.
Singular.

LINDSAY: Sorry…

MARK: Jesus Christ!

(*A silence.*)

LINDSAY: He nearly…

MARK: Anyway I played twice. Yeah? I played two games.
Two games. Twice.

LINDSAY: Twice. (*A long pause.*) He was their supersub.

MARK: Alright!

LINDSAY: Anyway, it's…

RUTH: I can't believe it. I'm really impressed.

(*A silence.*)

LINDSAY: He hit the post.

MARK: The crossbar!

LINDSAY: The crossbar.

RUTH: Is that good then?

MARK: What you mean?

LINDSAY: Well, it is rather better to score.

MARK: The ball crossed the line.

LINDSAY: Though the umpire said it didn't.

MARK: The referee!

LINDSAY: The referee, sorry.

MARK: And he was a blind twat, wasn't he?

> (*A silence.*)
> To be fair.

LINDSAY: Darling, I think you did terribly well…

RUTH: God, yes. To even hit a post.

MARK: The crossbar.

LINDSAY: And he was only on the field for the last ten minutes.

MARK: Five minutes!

LINDSAY: Five minutes, sorry.

> (*A silence.*)
> It's annoying really because if he'd have scored then they'd have won the game and the reserve league table, you see, and he would have been a bit of a hero but as it was…

MARK: I *did* score.

LINDSAY: That was the last game he… the last game he… the last…

> (*A silence.*)

RUTH: Look, please do help yourself to a nibble.

> (*MARK reaches across and does so.*)
> Lindsay?

LINDSAY: I'm alright for the moment, thanks.

MARK: Have something to eat, for God's sake!

LINDSAY: I'm not hungry, thank you.

MARK: No, you're never fucking hungry, are you?

> (*A silence.*)

RUTH: Now then…are you absolutely sure you wouldn't like a beer?

(*No answer. LINDSAY looks hard at MARK.*)

MARK: I'd love one, to be fair.

LINDSAY: Excuse me?

MARK: But I'm not allowed.

LINDSAY: He's driving.

MARK: She thinks I'm an alcoholic.

(*A silence.*)

LINDSAY: It's not a good idea.

MARK: I think it's a very good idea.

RUTH: Well, look, I'll get one and you can make up your minds as to whether or not you…yes. Yes, that's what I'll do.

(*RUTH leaves and enters the kitchen area. She gathers herself.*)

(*To herself.*) Stupid middle-class bitch? You're not.

LINDSAY: Honestly, if you swear at me like that again…

RUTH: (*To herself.*) You're not a middle-class bitch.

LINDSAY: And you are not drinking, please!

RUTH: (*To herself.*) Well, of course you are. Of course you bloody are.

LINDSAY: You've been doing really well, but please don't go back to…

RUTH: She left out 'fat', though, didn't she? Yes. She only went and left out the word 'fat'.

LINDSAY: Please don't drink. You get nasty when you drink.

(*RUTH pours herself a large wine and then gets a can from the fridge.*)

RUTH: (*To herself.*) Anyway who cares? Because tonight… tonight everything will finally come to an end… (*Drinks.*) Yes. The end. The end of the road.

LINDSAY: I'm asking you, Mark, for the last time…

(*No answer.*

LINDSAY, upset, stands up and walks away from the table.

RUTH comes onto the terrace with the can of lager and a glass.)

RUTH: There we go.

(*MARK takes the beer, puts it on the table. He stares at it for a time.*)

Everything alright?

MARK: Yes, thanks.

(*A tense silence.*)

RUTH: Everything alright over there?

LINDSAY: (*Back to them.*) Yes, thanks.

RUTH: Thank you both so much for coming.

(*A silence.*)

Good health then.

(*RUTH drinks.*

MARK studies the can on the table for a time.)

You don't like Stella Artois?

MARK: I absolutely…love it.

RUTH: Because I have something from the…

MARK: Also goes by the name of Wifebeater.

RUTH: …from the Czech Republic in the fridge if you prefer?

MARK: This is perfect.

(*He continues to stare at it. He then runs a finger lovingly down the side of the can.*

RUTH watches him for some time.

MARK continues to stare at the beer, with RUTH watching him.

LINDSAY, with her back to them, seems to be inspecting RUTH's flower pots. After a time:)

RUTH: Hope you approve of my little babies?

LINDSAY: Sorry?

RUTH: My plants. They do become a little like your babies, don't they, or at least your pets, after a time. Of course Mother was the real greenfingered one but she died recently so it's just me now and I'm sort of picking up where she left off.

LINDSAY: I'm sorry to hear…

RUTH: You see that old sycamore just there, I had a sort of treehouse up on the top branches when I was little and I used to hide up there…you know, when things got too unpleasant indoors. I'd go down there, climb up into the branches and I'd just…you know…have a good old scream, a good old weep.

(*A silence.*)

LINDSAY: (*Inspecting a dead plant.*) Well, I can see you clearly…

RUTH: It's so nice, isn't it, to watch things grow, it connects you with nature. I have this huge garden out there that I've absolutely no idea what to do with. It's just running wild really. But I do love to watch things grow but of course you know all about these things, about things growing, as you have your three children and your… Isn't it three?

LINDSAY: Charles, Emily and Ben.

RUTH: Oh, I know thousands of children called Emily.

(*A silence.*)

LINDSAY: Well, I suppose it is quite a popular…

RUTH: And hundreds of Bens.

(*A silence.*)

(*Drinks.*) Thank you both so much for coming.

(*She now watches MARK again as he considers the beer can.*)

Children and me. Just not meant to be. (*Laughs.*) Oh, what about that then? I'm a poet and I just don't know it.

(*She laughs.*

A strained smile from MARK. The silence builds.)

I have a friend… well, friend might be a little too strong and… well, I mean I like *her* but I don't know if she likes *me*…and anyway she has these two children and I love them dearly…well, maybe love's too strong a word…I find them quite…endearing, I suppose… but how you actually live with the things under your feet all day, I've no idea. Always demanding things aren't they and either crying or shouting or whingeing or…

MARK: Shitting.

(*A silence.*)

RUTH: Anyway…thank you both so much for coming.

(*A silence.*)

Okay, so…do you have photos or…?

(*MARK gets out his wallet and produces some small photographs. He hands them to RUTH who hands them back almost immediately.*)

How wonderful then.

MARK: You not married then?

RUTH: No.

MARK: Never been married?

RUTH: No.

MARK: Never wanted to be married?

RUTH: (*After a pause.*) No.

MARK: (*To LINDSAY.*) You never told me you had such a
sensible friend.

(*A silence.*)

RUTH: I see you're inspecting my avocado plant?

LINDSAY: Yes, but it's…

RUTH: Grew it from the stone.

LINDSAY: It doesn't seem to be all that…

RUTH: As I say, I do love to watch things grow.

LINDSAY: …alive.

(*A silence.*)

Well, Ruth, you have a lovely house.

RUTH: Thank you.

LINDSAY: And a lovely garden.

RUTH: It's really good to see you again.

LINDSAY: And it's good to…

RUTH: Thank you both so much for coming.

(*A long silence.*)

LINDSAY: I'm sorry about your mother, I… (*A pause.*) She was
a real fun-loving lady as I recall?

RUTH: (*Suddenly very serious.*) Oh, no, Lindsay. No. Not at all.
Not even remotely.

(*A long silence. She drinks.*)

You know, I was just thinking: all the water that's flown
under the bridge. We were such hopeful young girls,
weren't we, with the whole world waiting for us and such
optimism that we could go out there into it and take
whatever we wanted and all those limitless opportunities…

LINDSAY: Yes.

RUTH: (*After a pause.*) And now here we all are. Sort of…stuck.
Quickly and quietly becoming…well…middle-aged really.
Just stuck with our dull little…lives.

(*A silence. She drinks.*)

Just going through the motions really.

(*No answer.*)

But…no… I mean…what am I saying?… you've done well, haven't you? With your husband and your children and your…

LINDSAY: It's not all been a bed of roses actually.

RUTH: Oh, it has. For someone like you. Believe me, it really really has.

(*MARK now takes the can of beer in his hand and pours it slowly into the glass.*

LINDSAY and RUTH watch him.

He then very slowly brings the glass to his lips.

LINDSAY makes a move towards the kitchen, clearly upset. She enters the kitchen.)

Is everything alright?

MARK: Not really.

RUTH: You shouldn't be drinking?

MARK: No.

RUTH: I've been insensitive.

MARK: She'll be fine.

RUTH: Are you sure?

(*No answer.*)

Anyway… thank you both so much for coming.

(*MARK now drinks. It's the first one he's had for quite a while. He enjoys it a great deal.*)

MARK: Heaven.

RUTH: Really?

MARK: Absolute heaven.

RUTH: Well. I'm glad you're…

MARK: Bliss.

RUTH: …enjoying it.

(*A silence.*

He pours more beer.

She watches him.)

MARK: To be fair…we were expecting a different kind of evening.

RUTH: Thank you both so much for coming.

MARK: A little more…I don't know… busy.

RUTH: I see.

MARK: But it's just us, is it?.

RUTH: And then Caroline Denholm-Young. I'm keeping my
fingers crossed. Because she's so busy, you see.

MARK: A real jet-setter, is she?

RUTH: Oh, definitely.

(*A long awkward silence.*
LINDSAY in the kitchen is the picture of despair.
RUTH turns and heads for the kitchen.)

Everything alright in here?

LINDSAY: Yes. Thank you.

RUTH: Listen, I'm sorry if there's been a misunderstanding.
Your husband says you thought it was going to be some big
jamboree or something but no, I just wanted to catch up
with a few old friends.

LINDSAY: It's just your invite did say Garden Party and…

RUTH: Well, outside is the garden and I would say we're
having a party.

LINDSAY: It's fine. Honestly.

RUTH: Wouldn't you?

(*A silence.*)

Thank you both so much for coming.

LINDSAY: It's a…

RUTH: You have such a pretty face, you know. I used to be
rather… obsessed with you…I've had a few drinks now
so I feel I can be candid…. You looked so much like…so
much like my sister and… And it really upset me…you
know…that we lost touch. I felt I must have offended you
in some…

LINDSAY: Oh no, no…not at all…

RUTH: We sort of just drifted, didn't we? When we went to
university? It happens, doesn't it? You were getting on with
your life and I was getting on with mine. And boys and…
studying and…

LINDSAY: Well, I didn't do much of that.

RUTH: Studying or boys?

LINDSAY: Studying.

RUTH: No studying but lots of boys, was it?

LINDSAY: (*After a pause.*) Well…

RUTH: I was the other way round sadly.

LINDSAY: (*To herself almost.*) I rather threw away my education.

RUTH: And so here we both are. Having to live with all those choices we made.

(*No response.*)

Thank you both so much for coming.

(*A silence. They smile at each other.*)

I really didn't mean to cause a problem with your husband's…

LINDSAY: (*A subject change.*) I love your kitchen by the way.

RUTH: Thank you.

LINDSAY: It's really…lovely.

RUTH: Compact.

LINDSAY: Cosy.

RUTH: Does the job.

(*A silence. Outside MARK slowly crushes the empty can with his hand.*)

Anyway, thank you both so much for coming.

(*A massive silence. LINDSAY coughs.*

The doorbell eventually sounds.)

(*Laughing.*) Oh…there we go! Saved by the bell.

(*As RUTH leaves to answer the door, MARK comes into the kitchen.*

A tense atmosphere between him and his wife. He looks around the kitchen and then heads for the fridge.

LINDSAY watches him.

He opens the door of the fridge and takes out another can. He then opens it and takes a swig. He walks past her and then out again.

She sighs deeply and sadly.)

LINDSAY: (*To herself.*) Somebody please…please…take me away…

(*STEVE now comes into the kitchen. He is in his 40s, an ex-soldier. He's been to hell and back in his life. His experiences have left him with a speech impediment. Especially when confronted by strangers every word is a struggle.*

She has not noticed his entrance.

MARK is now wondering around the terrace area, swigging his beer, perhaps kicking around an old tennis ball that's lying about.

In the kitchen.)
STEVE: Alright?
   (*LINDSAY turns to face him. She's immediately taken by him.*)
   Lost my key… Leave a spare…with Ruth. Steve.
LINDSAY: (*After a pause.*) Lindsay.
   (*A silence.*)
STEVE: There's a…photographer…outside.
   (*She smiles back.*)
   Loitering…with…intent.
LINDSAY: With what, sorry?
STEVE: Any…VIPS…inside?
LINDSAY: I don't…don't really know. (*A pause.*) Sorry.
   (*A silence.*)
STEVE: Won't intrude…
LINDSAY: You won't be…
STEVE: What?
LINDSAY: Intruding.
STEVE: Right.
   (*A silence.*)
LINDSAY: Do we…do we know each other?
STEVE: No. I don't…
LINDSAY: It sort of feels like… I'm looking into the face of an
   old friend actually. You didn't go to the Boys' School then?
STEVE: No.
LINDSAY: Are you sure?
STEVE: Been…working as a… (*A very long pause as he struggles.*)
   …janitor, mind. Handyman. At the Girls' School.
LINDSAY: Oh, that's where I was…educated. In aeons past.
   (*A silence.*)
   Must be hard. Dishy man like you amongst all those eager
   young girlies?
   (*He does not respond. Smiles at her. She smiles back.*
   Now MARK comes into the kitchen area. They do not see him.
   Nobody speaks.)
MARK: Hope I'm not interrupting?
   (*A silence.*)
   You the footballer then?
LINDSAY: This is Steve.

(*STEVE tries to stammer out a greeting but fails.*)

MARK: (*To LINDSAY.*) Is he the footballer?

LINDSAY: (*To STEVE.*) Are you the footballer?

(*STEVE tries to stammer out an answer but fails.*)

MARK: (*To LINDSAY.*) Is he alright?

STEVE: No.

MARK: You're not alright?

STEVE: Not the…footballer.

LINDSAY: He doesn't look like a footballer.

STEVE: I… I….

(*MARK looks to his wife, clearly wrong-footed by STEVE's speech problem.*)

MARK: No, he doesn't. Bit old.

(*MARK walks across to the fridge.*)

Want a beer, mate?

STEVE: No….

MARK: (*To LINDSAY.*) What about you?

STEVE: …thank you.

(*No response from LINDSAY.*

They watch MARK as he takes out another beer. MARK swigs from it and stays where he is. Nobody speaks.)

So…if you're not the footballer, who are you?

STEVE: A…neighbour.

MARK: A neighbour, is it?

(*A silence.*)

A… (*Neighs the first syllable.*) …neigh-bour.

(*He laughs. It peters out. A long silence.*)

So…what do you do, now that we've established it isn't football?

STEVE: Was a…

LINDSAY: He works at the school.

STEVE: …soldier.

MARK: You know what they say about teaching?

STEVE: But now I'm a…

MARK: Those who can, teach. Those who can't…

STEVE: …writer.

MARK: No. Those who can't, do. Those who can…

LINDSAY: What kind of writer?

MARK: (*To LINDSAY.*) What is it?

STEVE: Suppose I can…say that now.

LINDSAY: Definitely fiction.

STEVE: I wouldn't…

MARK: Not a great reader of fiction myself, to be fair. (*To LINDSAY.*) Am I? Always end up thinking, what's the point? Someone's just made this bullshit up, so why am I bothering? You know what I mean? If there's no problem to solve or no fact to be learned then…

LINDSAY: What kind of fiction?

STEVE: It's not…

LINDSAY: Don't tell me…you write for children?

STEVE: Not…

LINDSAY: I knew it…

MARK: My wife tries her hand at that.

STEVE: I don't…

MARK: (*Laughing.*) Keeps her off the streets anyway!

STEVE: (*To LINDSAY.*) You write for…?

MARK: She tries, she tries…

STEVE: (*To LINDSAY.*) What age?

MARK: I'd say maybe five to seven-year-olds.

STEVE: (*To LINDSAY.*) My novel's about the horrors of…

MARK: She did one about a boss-eyed goat.

STEVE: …of warfare.

MARK: A boss-eyed goat with a spaccy speech impediment.
(*A terrible silence.*)

STEVE: Any…published?

LINDSAY: Oh God, no. I'm…

MARK: Just a hobby really.

STEVE: Maybe you should…send…some off?

LINDSAY: I…

MARK: She has.

STEVE: Well, that's good…

MARK: And they all just keep a-coming straight back.
(*A silence.*)
She illustrates as well.

STEVE: I'm…I'm… impressed.

LINDSAY: Don't be.

STEVE: Well, I am.

MARK: Well, he is.

LINDSAY: My current role is 'busy housewife and mother of three' so…

STEVE: But, surely writing…and …motherhood aren't…they aren't…

MARK: Mutually exclusive? No. They're not.

(*A silence.*)

Definitely not.

STEVE: You should…pers…

LINDSAY: What about you? Are you published?

STEVE: Well, as I say, last month I did get my first…

MARK: We buy loads of kids books. Well, the wife does. And the burning question is of course…do we have any of your masterworks upon our very shelves?

STEVE: Well, as I say, I don't…

MARK: Give us a title then.

STEVE: My book is about my time in the…

MARK: The only one I really like is *Halibut Harry*.

STEVE: …in the first Gulf War.

LINDSAY: *Halibut Harry* is awful.

STEVE: And my struggle to…

MARK: It's about a boy who turns into a fish.

STEVE: …deal with life…

LINDSAY: A halibut.

STEVE: …with civilian life afterwards.

MARK: And a halibut is a fish, isn't it?

LINDSAY: I know but…

MARK: And we have to read it every night.

LINDSAY: You mean *I* have to.

MARK: My wife has to.

LINDSAY: And sometimes I think you should try.

MARK: I do read to them.

LINDSAY: You never do.

MARK: It's a good story. To be fair.

LINDSAY: (*To STEVE.*) I quite like *Neville the Devil.*

MARK: Not in the same league.

LINDSAY: I prefer it to *Halibut Harry* but…

MARK: It hasn't even got a plot.

LINDSAY: The illustrations are…

MARK: *Halibut Harry* is much the better book. End of story.
(*A silence.*)
But you look at some of these kids' books and you think 'do people actually earn money making this shit up'? It's money for old rope, to be fair.

LINDSAY: There is money to be made from it.

MARK: Then I just wish you'd hurry up and make some.

LINDSAY: I am trying.

MARK: Been doing it for ten years, Dave. Not made a single fucking penny.
(*A very long and very awkward silence.*
STEVE clears his throat.
RUTH now comes in.)

RUTH: (*Laughs.*) You know what they say about kitchens and parties!

MARK: What's that then?

RUTH: (*Laughing.*) Well…kitchens…parties. You know what they say.
(*A silence.*)

STEVE: I don't suppose you …?

RUTH: Here.
(*She throws him a key.*)

STEVE: Better be off then…

LINDSAY: I'm sure Ruth won't mind if you stay.

RUTH: It's a private party. I'm sorry.

LINDSAY: Oh, that sounds a bit mean…
(*A silence.*)

STEVE: I don't want…

LINDSAY: Well, listen, Ruth…I for one would really like Steve to stay.

RUTH: Would you?

LINDSAY: I would.

RUTH: And what would Steve like?

STEVE: I don't want to…to gatecrash…

LINDSAY: Please. Please stay. I'm really enjoying your company. Actually. I really am. Sorry. And I'd really like it if you stayed. Just for a while. Just for a bit. So…well…just stay then. Please. Okay? That alright? That agreed? That alright with everyone?

(*Nobody speaks. They all look at her.*)

Thank you. Sorry. Yes. Thanks. Sorry.

SCENE 2

A little later. STEVE and LINDSAY are still in the kitchen area. MARK is sat at the table in the terrace with a number of empty beer cans around him. He is now quite drunk. CAROLINE, a well-dressed and elegant woman, stands close by, evidently bored by him and seeking escape.

MARK: Because I ate, drank and shat football, to be fair. It was my whole life. Football, beer and birds. All I cared about when I was younger. And I was good. I was a decent enough striker. In my day.

STEVE: Then a…breakdown afterwards.

LINDSAY: That's awful.

STEVE: The MoD left us all…on our own.

LINDSAY: That's really terrible.

STEVE: To fend for ourselves.

LINDSAY: Your poor man.

STEVE: There's thousands like me.

MARK: My teachers thought I had what it took and I did well. Signed forms with Orient when I left school.

STEVE: From that war and now this new one.

MARK: As I say, what young lad doesn't want to play football for a living?

STEVE: And the Falklands of course.

MARK: None that I can think of.

STEVE: Me wife couldn't deal with me. The nightmares, the drinking…

MARK: And it was like a happy dream. I was tipped for the top. And I played a couple of games for the reserves and… as I say, I scored in a game that was the title decider…you know, off the crossbar and then down over the line…

LINDSAY: Have you tried therapy?

STEVE: Spent a lot of time wishing I'd not survived it.…

MARK: I mean, the ball was clearly over the line, anyone could see but no...we had some fat geriatric who couldn't keep up with the play, huffing and puffing on the halfway line when I scored...

STEVE: I did become hard to live with and I did drink so...

LINDSAY: To have someone actually listening to you, it's so liberating...

STEVE: I was a broken man and she said that...

LINDSAY: Actually listening to your problems.

STEVE: She said that I...

LINDSAY: It's made such a difference to me.

MARK: I mean, how could he see from there? I was wheeling away in celebration, punching the air, team-mates climbing over me and then he goes and disallows it.

STEVE: She said I wasn't the...

LINDSAY: I've given it up now because he says it's an extravagance but...

STEVE: ...the same person.

MARK: So I go after the ref. End up butting him. Sent off and then banned. I mean, if we'd have won that game then... well, who knows?

STEVE: She said I was unable to... That I was unable to... that I was completely unable to...

LINDSAY: To what, sorry?

STEVE: Communicate.

LINDSAY: I see.

STEVE: My feelings. To express my...

LINDSAY: So...what did you actually do in this war of yours?

STEVE: I...

LINDSAY: Because I have to admit, I know next to nothing about it...

STEVE: I killed Iraqi lads.

MARK: I mean, I was young... I liked a drink, of course I did, and I liked going out and yes alright I went off the rails a bit.

LINDSAY: Well, at least you've had an adventure...

STEVE: (*With an extreme effort.*) I think the only people who really... appreciate this life...

LINDSAY: At least you've seen a bit of the world…

STEVE: …the wonder and beauty of this very short, precious life of ours…

CAROLINE: (*Not unkindly.*) Well, Mark, that…

STEVE: …are people who've nearly lost it. People who've sort of come back from the dead…

LINDSAY: I've done nothing at all with my life.

STEVE: As it were.

CAROLINE: But if you'll be kind enough to excuse me…

MARK: I put on a bit of weight and…didn't look after myself properly but I did have talent.

CAROLINE: I'm sure you did.

LINDSAY: And it's all just passing me by so quickly.

MARK: I did have talent.

STEVE: You have children.

CAROLINE: As I say…

MARK: Everyone said.

LINDSAY: Anyone can have children.

STEVE: Well, that's not always…

LINDSAY: And sometimes I envy people who don't.

STEVE: And sometimes…people who don't…

MARK: Then…before I knew it, wallop, I was out on my arse.

STEVE: …envy people like you who do.

MARK: They just left me. To fend for myself.

STEVE: I'm sure you're a great…mother.

MARK: There's millions like me. Blokes in jobs they hate who just never made the grade.

LINDSAY: My children have unhappy parents.

MARK: I mean, it's a cruel game.

LINDSAY: And that'll hurt them in the end.

MARK: A cruel game. To be fair.

CAROLINE: The whole of life is something of a cruel game, is it not?

MARK: You're not wrong there, sweetheart.

CAROLINE: I beg your pardon?

MARK: To be fair.

CAROLINE: Yes…well…some of us are destined to win.

MARK: Not by a long stretch of the imagination.

CAROLINE: And some of us are sadly condemned to lose.

MARK: So…your bloke…he kicks a ball about, does he?

CAROLINE: You could say that.

MARK: Well… I wish him well with it.

CAROLINE: (*After a pause.*) Thank you.

MARK: But it's tough, you know…to make it. To get there.

CAROLINE: (*After a pause.*) Yes. Quite.

MARK: You tell him.

CAROLINE: I shall.

MARK: He can have that free of charge.

CAROLINE: Most kind.

MARK: No, but good luck to him.

> (*CAROLINE is again looking round to see if someone's coming to rescue her. In the end she makes a move towards the kitchen, when:*)

A struggle, isn't it? Used to be a laugh sometimes, we used to have a riot together but now…

LINDSAY: We did used to have fun though.

MARK: …it's just all worry now and kids and bills and…

LINDSAY: He was always a bit of a lad of course but…

MARK: …I don't know, it's all suddenly got so heavy.

LINDSAY: But he's so unhappy now. Says he feels lonely.

MARK: Like I can see my whole life mapped out in front of me and it's the same every day. And it's all just work, work, work. All I ever do now is work. I mean, it's all any of us are doing these days, innit? Work. Work. Morning, noon and night. Work, work and more fucking work.

LINDSAY: I try to get him to talk to someone but…

MARK: There's got to be more to it than all this work surely.

CAROLINE: I would say our work defines who we are.

LINDSAY: And I think I do still love him but…

CAROLINE: But if we do what we love doing then it ceases to be work.

MARK: I mean, you know what these top footballers are on these days?

LINDSAY: He's always comparing his life with everyone else's.

CAROLINE: I have a vague idea, yes.

LINDSAY: Goes on and on about being a failure.

MARK: The England captain earns more in a single week than I do in five years. A single week. And that's without all the commercials and endorsements. That's five years of slog and anxiety and hiring and firing and backbiting and let-downs and tendering for contracts and getting some and not getting others and VAT bills and accounts…

STEVE: He's got *you*, hasn't he?

MARK: …compared to ninety minutes of doing what you love doing. Kicking a bloody ball about.

CAROLINE: There is a certain disparity, yes.

MARK: Alright, granted there's a bit of training thrown in but I mean I run my own business, I work like a dog, I employ twenty-odd people, I've got twenty-odd people under me, Caroline, and we work, and we compete, and we compete for contracts and you know…it gets exhausting, doesn't it…the fight…the fight to be better, to be cheaper, to be faster, and all our competitors going over to China for cheaper labour and cheaper parts and undercutting us all the time and the debt I've got into…you know…just to stay afloat…

STEVE: And that's not such a bad thing.

MARK: She has no idea of our debts.

CAROLINE: Does she not?

MARK: And she's insisting they all get the very best education.

LINDSAY: Not such a bad thing?

MARK: And in our area that's going to cost.

STEVE: Well. You're a beautiful woman.

MARK: And then of course there's this stupid bloody horse.

LINDSAY: Am I?

MARK: I mean, these young guys…to earn all that money just for playing a game…

LINDSAY: Am I really?

CAROLINE: Market forces, I'm afraid.

MARK: Don't talk to me about market forces.

LINDSAY: It's a long time since anyone's said anything like that.

STEVE: Don't believe you.

CAROLINE: But if you'll excuse me…

MARK: I'd do anything to be twenty-one again.

CAROLINE: Wouldn't we all?

MARK: I mean, her parents have money but I won't ask. I'm no beggar and I do have my dignity.

CAROLINE: Yes, I can see that.

MARK: They've always looked down their noses at me. Thinking I'm not good enough for her.

LINDSAY: So…sorry…do you find me attractive then?

MARK: But I work my bollocks off for that precious daughter of theirs.

CAROLINE: How nice.

MARK: Work my bollocks to the bone.

CAROLINE: I see…

MARK: Give her everything she wants. Always have done. Everything

CAROLINE: She's a lucky woman then.

MARK: And the worst thing is, you know, I could have made it. I know I could.

CAROLINE: Yes.

MARK: With the right guidance. The right support.

(RUTH comes into the kitchen in a state of excitement. She is drunker now.)

RUTH: This is amazing! I don't think I have ever had an important person in my house before. Someone actually interesting and important and famous and clever. Normally they have fights, don't they, celebrities and the paparazzi!? But Claude says it's better to give them what they want now or they'll just be climbing over the walls and ruining our evening.

(RUTH goes out onto the terrace, just as CAROLINE attempts another escape.)

Honestly…it's amazing. Normally they have fights, don't they, celebrities and the paparazzi!?

CAROLINE: Ruth, may I ask you a question?

RUTH: Of course.

CAROLINE: Where might everyone else be?

RUTH: Everyone else?

CAROLINE: I thought this was going to be some twenty-year reunion. For our class. I assumed things would be well under way by now?

RUTH: Just…a few…old friends…

CAROLINE: I appreciate that but…

LINDSAY: (*To STEVE.*) I believe I asked you a question.

RUTH: We were a such a gang, weren't we?

CAROLINE: We were?

STEVE: As I say…

RUTH: Ruth, Lindsay and Caroline… always together, always plotting something.

CAROLINE: I wouldn't say gang exactly…

RUTH: Ruth…Lindsay…Caroline.

LINDSAY: A simple yes or no will suffice.

CAROLINE: We've come a long way for this. I thought Claude would find it interesting. To see what life in the provinces is like but it seems, Ruth, you have lured us here under false pretences.

RUTH: We were such a gang.

CAROLINE: And to be quite honest I've got slightly better things to be doing with my time than…

RUTH: Ruth, Lindsay and Caroline… always together, always plotting something.

MARK: (*To RUTH.*) What do you mean, celebrities?
(*At this point we hear:*)

VOICES: (*Off.*) Claude! Claude! Just one more, mate! One more, Claude, if you'd be so kind…
(*CLAUDE now comes into the kitchen. He is an athletic, good-looking black man in his mid-20s. He is dressed in loose-fitting clothes and wears sandals. He clearly has both money and taste. His manner is one of humility but quiet self-assurance. He is softly-spoken and French.*)

CLAUDE: Good evening.

STEVE: Alright?

CLAUDE: I hope I am in the right place for the…reunion?

LINDSAY: I'm afraid you are.

CLAUDE: Claude Kabinda.

LINDSAY: I'm Lindsay and this is Steve.

CLAUDE: So… may I ask where is the party?

LINDSAY: This is it, I'm afraid.

CLAUDE: Well…okay…it is very nice to see you.

(*A silence.*)

LINDSAY: So…you must be the footballer?

CLAUDE: That is correct.

LINDSAY: You're Caroline's friend?

CLAUDE: We are friends, yes. For the moment we are also very excellent lovers.

(*A silence.*)

STEVE: And you play for a living?

CLAUDE: That is correct.

STEVE: Who do you play for? Not the local lot, is it?

CLAUDE: In these days I play for Chelsea.

(*A silence.*)

LINDSAY: Oh, and they're really good, aren't they?

CLAUDE: And also for France.

(*A silence.*)

From time to time.

LINDSAY: I'm afraid I know nothing at all about football.

STEVE: Nor do I.

LINDSAY: (*Impressed.*) Really?

STEVE: A problem for a bloke.

CLAUDE: So you do not know who is Claude Kabinda?

LINDSAY: No. Sorry.

STEVE: Especially where I come from.

(*CAROLINE sees he's arrived and comes through into the kitchen.*)

CAROLINE: I do apologise for this…but it seems we have been lured here under false pretences.

CLAUDE: I don't…

CAROLINE: I know a lovely pub not far away with a view of the sea and…

MARK: (*To RUTH.*) Who's a celebrity?

CAROLINE: And then we can go straight to the hotel and…

CLAUDE: …we have some very excellent sex.

(*CLAUDE laughs heartily.*
A silence.

RUTH *now comes back into the kitchen.*
MARK, glass in hand, stands and walks away, annoyed at being ignored.)

RUTH: (*To CLAUDE.*) You don't know what it means to me to meet an important and interesting person. I was just saying to myself last night…I've never actually met an important, interesting person before.

CLAUDE: I am not so interesting…

RUTH: Please, please, come through.

CAROLINE: I really think we'll be going, Ruth…

RUTH: This way, this way…

CLAUDE: (*To CAROLINE.*) Baby, we stay for a time…

CAROLINE: It's a traditional place with a log fire and…

CLAUDE: But I think it would not be courteous to our host…if we leave to now.

RUTH: *Ce ne serait que discourtois, mais aussi complètement déshonorant.*

CLAUDE: *Vous parlez français?*

RUTH: *Je parle français, j'enseigne le français, j'aime tout ce qui est français.*

CAROLINE: Claude?

RUTH: You don't speak French?

CAROLINE: Only the rusty O-level variety.

RUTH: Do you not think it the sexiest sound in the world? A Frenchman in full flow in his native tongue.
(*RUTH leads CLAUDE by the hand towards the terrace area. CAROLINE watches in irritation.*)

CLAUDE: (*As he passes STEVE and LINDSAY.*) I just want to say…you two seem to be a very excellent couple…you know…very much in love. It is very beautiful to see. I can feel the love you have for each other. *Vous… répandez le bonheur.* I know your life together will be very beautiful. (*Smiling, he gently pats STEVE's shoulder and follows RUTH outside.*)

RUTH: *Le jardin est…*

CLAUDE: *C'est charmant, charmant…*
(*MARK now turns and sees CLAUDE. He is unable to comprehend quite who he is seeing. His mouth open, he simply gawps.*)

(*To MARK.*) Good evening.
(*No response from the stunned MARK.*)
Claude Kabinda. (*To RUTH.*) *Il va bien?*
RUTH: *Il est tout à fait bourré.*
CLAUDE: *Il vacille.*
RUTH: *Nous sommes une nation des ivrognes.*
CLAUDE: (*Laughing.*) *Peut-être.*
RUTH: *Moi, je suis toujours ivre.* (*She drinks.*)
CAROLINE: I really am slightly annoyed about this.
LINDSAY: Yes, we thought it was going to be…
CAROLINE: And I have no recollection of us being a gang.
LINDSAY: We weren't really, we…
CAROLINE: You're Lesley Davies aren't you?
LINDSAY: Lindsay. A Davies then. A Johnson now.
CAROLINE: Well, it's good to see you again.
RUTH: *Et aussi…*
CLAUDE: Please… I want improve my English…
RUTH: This way then, this way…
(*RUTH leads CLAUDE past the still-gawping MARK and off into the garden.*)
CAROLINE: Well, don't take this the wrong way, but the years have actually improved you.
LINDSAY: (*After a pause.*) Thank you.
CAROLINE: You have a tremendous figure.
LINDSAY: Well…
CAROLINE: And I take it you've had children?
LINDSAY: Three.
CAROLINE: Yes, you've held onto it very well.
LINDSAY: Thank you…
CAROLINE: Well done you.
LINDSAY: And what about you? You're…
CAROLINE: I really don't know what she means about us all being good friends. I remember her being a little eccentric and rather annoying to be honest.
LINDSAY: I remember…
CAROLINE: But I don't recall ever having a real conversation with her.
LINDSAY: She was…

CAROLINE: She was always talking, wasn't she, always trying to be amusing.

LINDSAY: She was rather…

CAROLINE: And forever bursting into tears.

LINDSAY: That's right. She…

CAROLINE: And she's still a touch overweight, isn't she?

LINDSAY: She was always on the…heavy side…

CAROLINE: Not ventured very far afield in life, has she?

LINDSAY: But she's still an attractive…

CAROLINE: I mean, I really thought this might be rather fun.

LINDSAY: We actually thought that, yes, it might…

CAROLINE: I was looking forward to showing off my lovely young superstar to all those dull provincial girls we used to know.

LINDSAY: She did say that it was going to be a…

CAROLINE: Ghastly little town though, isn't it?

LINDSAY: Well…I don't know…

CAROLINE: And what about you? What do you do?

LINDSAY: (*A nervous laugh.*) Well, just a 'busy housewife and mother of three' actually so…

CAROLINE: A financially independent 'busy housewife and mother of three', one trusts?

LINDSAY: Well…

CAROLINE: You know, I've met women who still have to ask their husbands for money, who would totally break apart without a man in their lives and I have to say it makes me rather cross.

LINDSAY: I think though that when you have children…

CAROLINE: I see how they live and it baffles me.

LINDSAY: Yes.

CAROLINE: I work very hard, I travel around the world, I earn extremely good money and…

STEVE: I think maybe what she's saying is…

CAROLINE: I mean, I do honestly believe that these women who define themselves in terms of a man are putting the movement back decades.

LINDSAY: Yes, but maybe if…

CAROLINE: Now, listen…would you mind if I gave you a little advice?

LINDSAY: Advice?

CAROLINE: I do believe there's quite an attractive woman lurking about somewhere here but she really isn't making the most of herself at the moment, is she?

LINDSAY: Is she not?

CAROLINE: So…next time you're at home and are in front of your bedroom mirror what I would suggest you do is this: take a really good hard look at what you see and ask yourself a simple question. Ask yourself: who do I want to be for the rest of my life? Then the next thing you must do is take a good hard look at yourself from someone *else's* perspective. How does Lindsay Johnson come across to other people? How does she come across right now, for example? If you find you are probably stuck in a fashion rut, don't be too ashamed because a lot of women are. A lot of 'busy housewives', a lot of 'busy mothers of three' are in exactly the same boat as you and it's nobody's fault. You simply need to face up to it. We can all spend ages justifying our lives to other people to make ourselves feel okay, but if it begins to sound hollow, it really may be time to make a big change. Perhaps we're not getting what we want out of life – from our careers or from our relationships – and part of the problem can often be because of the way we present ourselves. So to take the plunge, any woman needs to make a total shift in attitude.

LINDSAY: (*Unsure.*) Do they?

CAROLINE: Tip one: you're making the mistake a lot of women make if their breasts are a bit saggy or rather flat, by wearing a bra that is simply too small for you. This tends to create unsightly bulges on your back. You should always, always, always pick the right-sized bra and then you just insert gel or silicone bits. Tip the second: some women really do not suit jeans, Lindsay. You have, I'm afraid to say, rather generous thighs but the big plus is that you also have quite a fabulous little waist so you should maybe find an alternative pair of trousers with wide legs in a casual fabric. I would suggest linen in the summer and a fine needle tweed in the winter. Now, finally, it's quite clear to me that you're not exactly from the Bold and Beautiful camp so I won't be recommending you go for any sleeveless deep-necked strapless numbers but I do think for the shy and introverted wallflower such as yourself a boat-necked saree with a squared necked blouse is often just the ticket. (*Reaching for a bottle of wine.*) I assume our hostess won't mind if I help myself to a glass of this. Oh, dear God…it's from the New World!

LINDSAY: I'm afraid we…brought that.

CAROLINE: Has she nothing French?

(*A long silence as CAROLINE hunts for another bottle.*)

By the way, avoid the man outside at all costs. He is horribly inebriated, fearsomely dull and simply never stops talking.

LINDSAY: Well, he's probably just…

CAROLINE: And so how long have you two been together?

STEVE: Well, we're not…

CAROLINE: This'll do. (*Hands a bottle and a corkscrew to STEVE.*) Would you be so kind, darling?

(*STEVE starts to open the bottle.*)

LINDSAY: So…how did you meet your footballer? He seems to be…

CAROLINE: Do you know, I don't know what I've done to deserve it, but not only is Claude one of the most beautiful men in the world, it would appear that he is also one of the best footballers.

LINDSAY: Quite a catch then?

CAROLINE: Women crawling all over him of course, when I first met him, but I plucked him away from them with considerable expertise.

LINDSAY: Clever you.

CAROLINE: For a footballer he is very intelligent and also a little religious, which is rather quaint. He also appreciates art.

LINDSAY: As I say he…

CAROLINE: And he is so athletic. I mean, I'm sure you can imagine, it's a real treat to have sexual intercourse with a man like Claude Kabinda.

(*A long silence. LINDSAY clears her throat.*)

STEVE: And will you marry or…?

CAROLINE: You know, I do feel something is in the air. That some plan is being hatched. The boy has been acting very strangely all day. Mysteriously disappearing to make secret phone calls and I just have this happy feeling that… (*To STEVE.*) Are you struggling with that, my darling?

(*CAROLINE and LINDSAY watch STEVE as he struggles with the bottle and he eventually manages to pour CAROLINE a glass of wine.*)

Bless you.

STEVE: (*To LINDSAY.*) For you?

LINDSAY: Why the hell not?

(*LINDSAY knocks hers back in one. They then smile politely at one another.*)

So… when did you…?

CAROLINE: Do excuse me, won't you?

(*CAROLINE now steps back outside.*)

(*Calling off.*) Claude! Are you ready?

MARK: (*Turning, drunk.*) Kabinda.

CAROLINE: Excuse me?

MARK: Kabinda. Claude.

CAROLINE: Indeed.

MARK: Kabinda. Here. Garden.

CAROLINE: (*Calling off.*) Claude!!

MARK: Striker. Chelsea. Signed for.

CAROLINE: (*Calling off.*) Are you ready?!

MARK: Fifteen million.

LINDSAY: She's so elegant. So…poised.

STEVE: She's nothing on you.

LINDSAY: Listen, do you really find me attractive then?

(*Outside CLAUDE and RUTH now emerge back onto the terrace.*)

CLAUDE: Because, Ruth, inside you are a beautiful person. You tell me you are unhappy and you are lonely but no…it is just a question of how you look at life. You are looking at it in the wrong way.

CAROLINE: Darling, are you ready?

CLAUDE: There is beauty and there is love inside all of us. God loves you, Ruth, but you do not yet know it.

CAROLINE: Darling, I don't want to be…insensitive…but…

CLAUDE: I am having a nice time, baby. I talk to Ruth.

LINDSAY: I feel strangely close to you.

MARK: Kabinda.

LINDSAY: My heart's pounding like mad actually.

MARK: Kabinda.

CLAUDE: Excuse me?

MARK: You're Claude Kabinda.

CLAUDE: I know this, my friend.

RUTH: Can I get you some wine?

CAROLINE: He doesn't drink.

MARK: You're Claude Kabinda.

CLAUDE: This I know.

MARK: *The* Claude Kabinda.

CAROLINE: Claude.

LINDSAY: Can I ask you something?

CLAUDE: It is good for me to spend some time with these everyday people. (*Breathing in deeply.*) Ah, the smell of the air is so…beautiful.

MARK: You're Claude Kabinda.

CLAUDE: I feel so happy to be alive tonight.

LINDSAY: Please will you kiss me?

CLAUDE: God is smiling down on each and every one of us.
(*In the kitchen, STEVE and LINDSAY are very close.*)

MARK: (*Barely audible.*) Need the bog.

RUTH/STEVE: I beg your pardon?

MARK: Need the shit-house, the bog.

RUTH: Through the kitchen and then up the stairs.
(*MARK now drunkenly backs towards the kitchen, not taking his eyes off CLAUDE for a second, just as LINDSAY comes toward STEVE and a possible kiss.*)

End of Act One.

Act Two

SCENE 1

Moments later. MARK backing towards the kitchen. CLAUDE holding his hand out to CAROLINE.

MARK: Kabinda!

CLAUDE: Come, baby…I show you.

CAROLINE: Well, extraordinarily briefly then…

    (*Hand in hand, CLAUDE and CAROLINE exit to the garden.*)

MARK: (*Still dazed, entering the kitchen backwards.*) Kabinda!

    (*STEVE pulls away from LINDSAY quickly.*)

    He's Claude Kabinda.

LINDSAY: Really?

MARK: Can't believe it.

    (*MARK backs through the kitchen and exits.*

    A silence in the kitchen. In hushed tones:)

STEVE: I'm sorry…

LINDSAY: No. I'm sorry.

STEVE: I only came round to…

LINDSAY: But don't you want to?

STEVE: Under other circumstances…

LINDSAY: Have I just made a complete fool of myself?

STEVE: No…

LINDSAY: I have, haven't I?

    (*STEVE makes a move towards the terrace.*)

STEVE: If you'll excuse…

LINDSAY: Mark is such a problem.

    (*STEVE stops.*)

    And I feel somehow responsible. For his unhappiness.

STEVE: Maybe…

LINDSAY: It's all so hard, isn't it?

STEVE: Can be. Finding the right…life. Job, partner. The right…place to be.

    (*A silence.*

    STEVE makes another move towards the terrace.)

LINDSAY: Maybe I should just leave? Might be the kick up the arse he needs.

STEVE: I don't want to be…

LINDSAY: I just feel like I'm going mad. My life is so…I don't know…boring. It's just children and the school run and housework and Mark is always so miserable and…

STEVE: …but I just need to speak to…

LINDSAY: I mean, I know I shouldn't complain but…

STEVE: …and then I'll…

LINDSAY: I do of course realise that half the people in the world are starving to death.

STEVE: So…

LINDSAY: But I really can't believe that this is it, you know. This is my life. This. This. This is all it is. All it will ever be. (*STEVE now sees his opportunity and makes a move to the terrace. He comes outside. He watches a sad RUTH, who is seated at the table. He keeps thinking about addressing her but doesn't. LINDSAY has not noticed that she is now alone in the kitchen.*) I just feel so anonymous. So alone. I don't feel part of the world at all. Don't feel connected. In any way, shape or form. Being at home all day does tend to isolate you a bit. Mark says I should get a job but what's the point in having kids and then dumping them in a nursery? I do want to be there for them. And I think I'm quite a good mother. I'm not good at much in this life but I do believe that. And you should try looking after three children. It's not exactly easy. And I've never known what I wanted to do anyway. Never really been that interested in anything. Not like Caroline with her fashion or Ruth with her teaching or you with your…your army and your…war. It's so important, isn't it? To have a passion in life. If you don't have a passion or an interest or something to be enthusiastic about…well, I suppose you're just a bit lost really. Aren't you? I do write these stories I suppose but I know they're utter rubbish really. I've always been a bit directionless and lacking in confidence…my parents always told me I was adrift and lazy and that I wouldn't amount to much…so now…and you'll probably laugh at this…but I've been taking this assertiveness training. But Mark says that now I'm assertive at all the wrong times and about things that don't really matter very much and I was going to use tonight as a bit of a test, I suppose. See how I've been progressing with it. Put it all into practice, so to speak. But I'm quite ashamed of what I've just done, you know, hurling myself at you like that but... Oh, I don't know, I've had a bit too much to drink, I expect and if I'm really honest I think I started a family because I had absolutely no idea what else to do with myself. I suppose I thought it might give me some sort of a focus. Anyway now...now I think I'm quite ready for an affair. Actually. I mean, what's the harm in it anyway? It's absurd to think you can be with just one person for a whole lifetime, isn't it? I mean, whoever put that idea into people's heads in the first place? They want shooting. Mark says it's because we all live too long now...we should all be dead by forty like our ancestors and then we wouldn't have to spend decades and decades having to put up with each other like this. Anyway if I had an affair of some description then maybe I could summon up the courage to just clear off. Take the kids off somewhere. Or maybe get him to move in with his brother, I don't know. Because I know I bore him and he bores me and we're both just so bored and I always just feel so bored and so boring and so...missing out on everything really. And I realised something awful a while ago, it struck me like a bolt from the blue: I don't have any friends. I'm almost forty, Steve, and I just don't have any good friends at all.

(*On the terrace:*)

STEVE: Who *are* these people, Ruth?

LINDSAY: And it's odd because for the last year I've been trying to track down my old classmates without much success so when I got the invitation to come here....well, I jumped at it really. And now...I have to be honest...I'm really rather glad I came.

RUTH: I don't know.

STEVE: What are they doing here?

(*RUTH drinks.*)

And I'm worried about your drinking...

RUTH: You sound like my mother.

STEVE: Since all this…you know…since she…

RUTH: Exactly like her.

STEVE: You've really got to… You have to start…

RUTH: Start what?

STEVE: Being kinder to yourself…

RUTH: Go home.

STEVE: The booze makes everything seem worse than…

RUTH: Nothing worse than a reformed drinker…

STEVE: And I wanted to ask you…

RUTH: I'm preparing a little surprise.

STEVE: Ask you a question.

RUTH: And I really want you to go now.

(*Back in the kitchen.*)

LINDSAY: So, listen…what about giving me a quick tour of your bookshelves then?

(*She turns to see she is alone, while back outside.*)

RUTH: I miss my Mum. Even though she hated me.

STEVE: She didn't.

RUTH: I don't know what to do with myself now.

STEVE: Maybe it's time to…

RUTH: I've been so…left behind.

STEVE: But now you're…

RUTH: Last week I broke a chair. Been in the family for a hundred years. I sat down and the thing just burst into splinters beneath me.

STEVE: But maybe now it's time to live for yourself…

RUTH: But sometimes I just have to…eat.

STEVE: There's a world out there.

RUTH: And I have no place in it.

STEVE: And I was wondering if…

(*LINDSAY now comes out onto the terrace.*)

LINDSAY: Do you always abandon your women like that?

STEVE: Sorry?

LINDSAY: I feel rather offended actually.

STEVE: Sorry, I just had to have a quick word with…

(*From the garden we now easily hear the lowered offstage voices of CLAUDE and CAROLINE.*)

CLAUDE: (*Off.*) But it is good for me! To talk with these people.

CAROLINE: (*Off.*) But we have been lured here under false pretences!

CLAUDE: (*Off.*) I do not know what are these pretences!

CAROLINE: (*Off.*) I want to go!

CLAUDE: (*Off.*) But I think we stay!

CAROLINE: (*Off.*) But they are all so dull…

CLAUDE: (*Off.*) So why did we come?

CAROLINE: (*Off.*) I thought it might be fun.

CLAUDE: (*Off.*) The couple in the kitchen…

CAROLINE: (*Off.*) They're not a couple.

CLAUDE: (*Off.*) They do not even know of Claude Kabinda.

CAROLINE: (*Off.*) Lesley Davies is married to the drunk.

CLAUDE: (*Off.*) But these people are your friends?

CAROLINE: (*Off, laughing.*) Oh for God's sake, Claude, my friends!? Don't be so ridiculous!

CLAUDE: (*Off.*) We must be kind, baby. We maybe have better lives than they…

CAROLINE: (*Off.*) And the reason we do is because we've worked bloody hard for them. Got out into the real world and fought hard. They've just sat about expecting good times to happen and so now because they haven't…

CLAUDE: (*Off.*) We are the lucky ones.

CAROLINE: (*Off.*) Did they grow up in a slum like you did? Did they grow up on the streets? Were they bullied and abused all their lives like you were?

CLAUDE: (*Off.*) Okay…

CAROLINE: (*Off.*) The answer is of course a resounding NO!

CLAUDE: (*Off.*) Please…we maybe not speak so loud!

CAROLINE: (*Off.*) They are just four little failures and that's all that they are!

(*A long silence on the terrace.*
Then CLAUDE and CAROLINE eventually come on.
Nobody speaks for a time until:)

CAROLINE: Well, Ruth. It really is a… It really is a…

(*She senses an atmosphere.*)

…a lovely garden.

(*No response. The silence builds.*)

Well, anyway. It really has been nice to see you all again…

RUTH: I have a surprise for you.

CAROLINE: That's very sweet of you but we do have to check into our…

CLAUDE: But we agree to stay.

CAROLINE: No, darling. We just agreed that we would go.

CLAUDE: I think we come all this way and…

RUTH: Can I get anyone a drink then?

CLAUDE: A glass of water will be very good.

CAROLINE: Claude, no, no, no!

RUTH: Same again?

(*RUTH now leaves for the kitchen and starts sorting the drinks.*
CAROLINE sits in a foul temper, arms folded across her chest.
A long silence builds outside.
STEVE eventually escapes back to the kitchen.)

STEVE: Don't you think you ought to lay off the drink now?

RUTH: I'm entertaining.

STEVE: It depresses you.

RUTH: I am as always thoroughly entertaining.

(*A hugely long silence outside which is broken when CLAUDE's*
phone rings.)

CLAUDE: Excuse me.

(*He walks off into the garden with it.*)

RUTH: You seem so alone in the world.

STEVE: I like being on me own.

(*On the terrace:*)

LINDSAY: Looks like there's to be no escape then?

(*CAROLINE shoots her a filthy look.*
In the kitchen:)

RUTH: You should get yourself another wife, Steve.

STEVE: Maybe.

RUTH: Have some kids. You'd make a great father.

(*On the terrace:*)

LINDSAY: So I assume you live in London then?

CAROLINE: Where else in this horrible little country could one possibly live?

(*In the kitchen:*)

STEVE: When I came back…she told me 'I don't do, sad, Steve. I don't do dark and I don't do despair.' But you,

Ruth… you're different… you're… (*He breaks off.*) So,
what…are you planning on going on holiday?

RUTH: In a manner of speaking.

(*On the terrace:*)

CAROLINE: How people survive in the provinces I have no
idea.

(*In the kitchen:*)

RUTH: I've tried so hard to do the right thing. To care. For
people. For society. My parents believed you had to serve
the public. I've worked so hard and up every morning of
my life at seven and trying to help others all day and now
I've got nothing. No-one.

STEVE: You've just been…

RUTH: Look at everyone else. So good at it. Take it all in
their stride. They've got everything. Look at them all.
Everything.

(*On the terrace:*)

CAROLINE: Yes, it must be hell for you

LINDSAY: Well…

CAROLINE: Sheer hell on earth.

(*In the kitchen:*)

RUTH: (*Passing him a glass of water.*) Take this, please.

STEVE: It's just you've never mentioned these people before.

RUTH: Old friends.

STEVE: But you don't seem close.

RUTH: We're not.

(*On the terrace:*)

CAROLINE: Look what it's done to her. Staying in this
wretched little town all her life. Just looks what it's done.
As I say, how people live anywhere other than a big city I
have absolutely no idea.

LINDSAY: Mark does miss London terribly. I suppose that's
my fault too as…

CAROLINE: I hope you don't mind me saying this but
whenever I stumble across a fellow woman who's clearly
not fulfilling her potential then I always feel duty-bound to
step in and come to the rescue.

(*In the kitchen:*)

RUTH: I see couples together and I compare my life with theirs…

STEVE: The thing is not to compare…

CAROLINE: Success and happiness, Lindsay, is all about setting goals. It's all about making targets for ourselves and then reaching those targets. It's about saying 'in five years' time I want to be in such-and-such a place, in ten years' time I want to be here, I want to be there, or I want to have paid off the mortgage, or have trekked up the Himalayas, or have written a novel, or have learned to speak Spanish.' It's about setting yourself a goal and then working bloody hard to achieve it.

RUTH: I've failed.

CAROLINE: Just look at the wonderful Claude. He has the world at his feet.

LINDSAY: But he's been born with talent.

CAROLINE: But it's not just about talent, darling, it's more about the setting of goals.

LINDSAY: If you're born without much talent to speak of then life certainly is a bit of a…can be a bit of a slog. If you're just…

CAROLINE: Listen, what I tell any woman who is languishing in a state of either self-pity or self-doubt, what I tell her to do is this: write down on a piece of paper a list. A list of goals: small goals, large goals, old goals, failed goals and current goals. I tell her to make a very complete list.

STEVE: Maybe it's not failure. Maybe you just don't fit in.

CAROLINE: Circle with a red marker pen those goals that interest you the most.

STEVE: And that's what you're calling 'failure'.

CAROLINE: Cross out the goals that don't especially interest or excite you.

STEVE: And maybe that's not such a bad thing: to be unable to fit into the way this world works, the way it's been set up.

CAROLINE: Then you must add new, desirable goals. Really push the envelope of your self-limitations and set goals that you really, really want. What are your greatest desires, Lindsay? What are your greatest dreams?

STEVE: Maybe this feeling of failure is just a way of life
suggesting a new path for you.

CAROLINE: If you had unlimited time, money and support,
what would your life be like?

STEVE: A door to a better way.

CAROLINE: What would you do? What would you have?

STEVE: A slower way, maybe. A simpler way.

CAROLINE: If you knew you could accomplish anything at all,
what would your goals be?

STEVE: All is vanity, Ruth. Remember. All is vanity.

LINDSAY: Well, I suppose I'd…

CAROLINE: (*Looking off into the garden.*) Oh, is he not done
yet? We agreed, we said today… we'd both turn our
phones off for the whole day. Have a day just for us. A day
uninterrupted. (*Calling.*) Claude!
(*In the kitchen.*)

RUTH: But at school, Steve…at school.

STEVE: I know…

RUTH: (*Head dropping.*) Everyone was just so…

STEVE: Ask these people to go.

RUTH: People used to say such…dreadful things.

STEVE: They don't now though, do they?

RUTH: They sacked me, Steve. You any idea at all how bad
that feels?
(*LINDSAY now comes inside again.*
STEVE smiles politely, RUTH holds onto a cupboard.
MARK now comes on from the hall, more drunk.
*RUTH is behind him, fixing drinks with difficulty and he does
not see her.*)

MARK: Had a snoop round the house, Lindse. Unbelievable.
Her room, it's like a teenager's. She's still got posters
of pop stars and horses all over the place and this big
pink panda on her bed and teddy bears everywhere. It's
like…Jesus Christ…she must be retarded or something. I
mean, what is she? Our age? I've never seen anything like
it. I mean, it's cheered me up, to be fair. I thought we were
a pair of losers but I can tell you something: we've got
absolutely nothing on her.

(*A terrible silence as* MARK *realises that* RUTH *is in the room.*)
(*To* RUTH, *barely audible.*) Alright?

RUTH: That room belonged to my sister. She died when she was eleven.

(RUTH, *upset, exits off to the hall.*
A long silence.)

MARK: Shit.

LINDSAY: For God's sake, Mark…

MARK: Have I upset her?

LINDSAY: Go and say sorry.

(STEVE *makes a move to follow* RUTH.
MARK *stops him and holds him by the arm.*)

MARK: I didn't mean to upset her.

STEVE: If you'll excuse me…

MARK: I had no idea. Didn't see her there.

STEVE: I think I'd better just…

MARK: I'm really sorry.

LINDSAY: Please. Go and say you're sorry.

MARK: I will.

STEVE: Perhaps, if I could…

MARK: I really love this wife, Steve.

LINDSAY: Not now, Mark…

MARK: This wife. This woman.

LINDSAY: Mark…

MARK: Look at her. She's a bit of alright, isn't she?

STEVE: I think I'd better…

MARK: Gorgeous. Isn't she?

STEVE: I think Ruth's a bit…

MARK: Don't you think?

STEVE: Well…

MARK: Don't you think she's gorgeous?

STEVE: If you'd just let go of me…

MARK: She's my wife, she is. My wife. My woman.

STEVE: She is.

MARK: Would you not say that I'm a lucky man?

LINDSAY: Mark, please…

MARK: I want to hear him say it.

LINDSAY: Please…

MARK: I want to hear him say it. Come on. You think she's
    gorgeous, don't you?

STEVE: Well, as I say…

MARK: Go on. I want you to say it.

    (*A silence.*)

    I'm waiting.

STEVE: She is a very…well, what can I say? Yes. She's a…she's
    a very attractive woman. Yes.

MARK: Very attractive?

STEVE: I'm sorry, I'd really like to…

MARK: But not gorgeous?

LINDSAY: For God's sake…

MARK: This is my wife.

STEVE: Yes.

MARK: My wife. And I love her.

STEVE: Yes.

MARK: I love her more than you will ever know, Steve. More
    than any book. To be fair. I love her more than any one of
    your…any one of your funny little children's books.

STEVE: I see.

MARK: You see, do you?

    (*No response. MARK sways a little.*)

STEVE: So…would you let go of me arm, please?

MARK: Sorry?

STEVE: Would you let go of me arm…?

MARK: (*Arm around her as well as around STEVE.*) And I'm sorry.
    Really. For the way I've been. I'm going to try harder. I
    mean it.

LINDSAY: Your breath stinks.

MARK: I'm going to make things right. I mean, I'm going to…
    I mean, I just love her, mate. I just really, really love her.

STEVE: Did you hear?

MARK: Kabinda.

STEVE: Sorry?

MARK: Kabinda. Claude Kabinda. Out there. Can't believe it.

    (*MARK releases STEVE and LINDSAY and staggers off onto the
    terrace. When he gets there he sways some more and watches
    CAROLINE, who is still seated.*)

STEVE: So…if you'll…

LINDSAY: Steve…I want you to take me to your flat.

STEVE: Sorry?

LINDSAY: I want you to show me where you work.

STEVE: It's just a rented flat and a computer…

LINDSAY: So…lets go there, please. You and me. Right now.
(*A silence.*)

STEVE: I'm sorry, but…

LINDSAY: This is not something I am in the habit of doing, I can assure you and I never normally behave in this way but…

STEVE: I just came here to…

LINDSAY: But I am now setting myself a goal.

STEVE: A goal?

LINDSAY: Since you seem to be rather slow on the uptake, I'll spell it out for you, shall I?

STEVE: Listen…

LINDSAY: I am attracted to you and it seems that you are attracted to me. So what I suggest is that we go across to your flat right now, we undress each other with some haste and then we have some energetic and utterly uncomplicated sex.
(*On the terrace:*)

MARK: Kabinda.

CAROLINE: (*Turning.*) I beg your pardon?

MARK: He's Claude Kabinda.
(*MARK now exits off into the garden area.
In the kitchen:*)

LINDSAY: I won't make any demands, I promise. I'll just go back to my boring little existence. And you can go back to yours.

STEVE: Listen, sorry…

LINDSAY: I just need some excitement please, Steve. For once in my life. I just really need to have some bloody excitement, please.
(*A silence.*)
Sorry, you're not a homosexual, are you?
(*A silence.*)

You are, aren't you?
(*STEVE hesitates.*
LINDSAY bursts out laughing.)
Oh my God, I'm so, so sorry.

STEVE: So…if you'll excuse me…

LINDSAY: Of course you are! It all makes perfect sense now.

STEVE: Well…

LINDSAY: Why on earth didn't you say?

STEVE: Look, I'm not actually…

LINDSAY: You've just been standing there all this time, watching me digging myself further and further into this big, bloody embarrassing hole.
(*She continues to laugh.*)

STEVE: Sorry. I'm not. Gay. No. Sorry.
(*Her laughter peters out.*)

LINDSAY: So…you're not?

STEVE: No.

LINDSAY: You're not gay?

STEVE: Not at all.

LINDSAY: Not at all gay?

STEVE: Not at all gay.

LINDSAY: Not even remotely gay?

STEVE: Not even remotely gay.

LINDSAY: (*After a pause.*) Are you sure?

STEVE: Quite sure.

LINDSAY: So, why then don't you want to…?

STEVE: If you'll excuse me…

LINDSAY: It can't be…her, surely? You can't be…? I mean you two aren't…? You don't surely have a thing for…? Oh my God…
(*STEVE finally gets away and rushes off to the hall.*
A long silence.)
(*To herself.*) You stupid, stupid, stupid, stupid, stupid, stupid, stupid, stupid, stupid, stupid…
(*On the terrace CAROLINE now stands. She comes into the kitchen. She stops and watches LINDSAY from behind.*
LINDSAY now has her hands over her head and rocks slightly.)

What are you doing with your life, you stupid woman? What the hell are you doing with your life? What are you doing here? What are you doing here? What on earth are you doing here?

CAROLINE: My sentiments exactly.

(*LINDSAY looks up.*)

It is my firm intention now to locate my coat.

(*CAROLINE exits to the hall.*

LINDSAY now sits at the kitchen table, a picture of misery.

Outside CLAUDE and MARK come onto the terrace, CLAUDE with his arm around MARK's shoulder.)

CLAUDE: Because like I say, Mr Mark, you have many things to be happy for.

MARK: I do?

CLAUDE: Of course.

MARK: You're Claude Kabinda.

CLAUDE: (*Laughing.*) This I know.

MARK: I can't believe it.

CLAUDE: You must believe.

MARK: You're Claude Kabinda.

CLAUDE: You have a good business, you have three children, you have a beautiful wife, you have…

MARK: You think she's beautiful then?

CLAUDE: You are joking with me, yes?

MARK: You really think she's beautiful?

CLAUDE: Between you and me, you know…man to man… your wife, she is absolutely my type.

MARK: Really?

CLAUDE: How do you say? She is my cup of tea, yes?

MARK: Can't believe it.

CLAUDE: The body is…like perfection.

MARK: Really?

CLAUDE: For sure. Women must be thin. It is so important. I like these models very much. Yes, she is…out of this world for me.

MARK: But Caroline is…

CLAUDE: Caroline is good, yes, but… your wife, she… I mean, really…

MARK: Caroline is class.

CLAUDE: You think so?

MARK: To be fair.

CLAUDE: They are both very fine women.

MARK: A woman like Caroline. Way out of my league.

CLAUDE: I think you do very well.

MARK: Never cheated on her.

CLAUDE: Well, I'm afraid I am…what you might say…a very
    bad boy.

MARK: You're Claude Kabinda.

CLAUDE: You know, and I always prefer the older woman.
    She has much more experience. You know. In the
    bedroom. And to talk with she is much more…interesting.

MARK: I mean, what…would you want to sleep with her then?

CLAUDE: Excuse me?

MARK: Is she the sort of woman you'd actually like to…

CLAUDE: (*Laughing.*) Well, yes. Why not? If she was…*libre*…
    available.
    (*A silence.*)

MARK: I can't believe it!

CLAUDE: But she is all yours, my friend!

MARK: Claude Kabinda wants to…with my wife!

CLAUDE: Not so loud, please…

MARK: I can't believe it! It's like a happy, happy dream!

CLAUDE: (*Laughing.*) This is man to man, I think.

MARK: Claude Kabinda wants to… My wife… He actually
    wants to…

CLAUDE: (*Laughing.*) Mr Mark, she will hear!

MARK: I can't believe it.

CLAUDE: But, as I say, she is not *libre* so…

MARK: You wouldn't… I mean, an autograph. Can't wait to
    tell my…can't wait to tell my…tell my…tell my little boy.

CLAUDE: Tell him what?

MARK: He's a big fan.
    (*MARK starts emptying his pockets. After a very long search, with
    much debris falling out, he locates a receipt and a pen. He hands
    them to CLAUDE.
    CLAUDE writes.*)

CLAUDE: Okay, Mr Mark… I tell you what I do.

MARK: You really think she's sexy?

CLAUDE: Listen to me…

MARK: I mean, would you really want to sleep with her then?

CLAUDE: I want to help you, my friend. I am a Christian man and I like to help people.

MARK To help people?

CLAUDE: But you must promise me that you will look after yourself, yes? You will stop all this drinking and gambling and you will take care of your beautiful wife. Look to the Lord for guidance.

MARK: You're Claude Kabinda.

CLAUDE: This I know.

MARK: Striker.

CLAUDE: You are with me?

MARK: Always. Always.

CLAUDE: And you must also pray for me, yes? When the World Cup begins?

MARK: I'll pray.

CLAUDE: You must pray I will have a good tournament.

MARK: Some of your goals are so…

CLAUDE: You like my goals?

MARK: It's like magic.

CLAUDE: God has blessed me with these majestic foots.

MARK: Insured for a million.

CLAUDE: (*Laughing.*) You have done your homework, my friend.

MARK: I can't believe I'm… I mean, is it really you?

CLAUDE: Here…

MARK: It's like a happy happy dream.

(*CLAUDE returns the receipt and pen to MARK.*)

CLAUDE: I want you to write down your bank numbers. You say you need money for your daughter's horse? Well, Claude Kabinda…he will help you. Write.

(*MARK writes.*)

MARK: I don't understand.

CLAUDE: You tell me you struggle?

MARK: I do. I struggle.

CLAUDE: Okay so…in the next days, I give the money for you. This is not a problem for me. It is for me…how do you say…small peanuts.
(*A long silence. MARK is stunned.*)
You are a good man, I think.

MARK: Am I?

CLAUDE: Underneath.

MARK: You would do that for me?

CLAUDE: You are a schoolfriend with Caroline?

MARK: Well, my wife…

CLAUDE: Because I finish it tonight. You understand? I speak with another of my girls just now and she is angry. (*Laughs.*) She does not like to share Claude Kabinda.

MARK: I see.

CLAUDE: So, I'm sorry to hurt your friend but you will take care of her, yes?

MARK: Of course.

CLAUDE: This is all I ask.

MARK: Of course.

CLAUDE: She can…be very…how to say… *émotive.*

MARK: Thank you so much.
(*MARK hands the paper to CLAUDE.*)

CLAUDE: Leave this to me. (*Pocketing it.*) I tell you, my friend, when you have the big money, this life it is…oh it is just so very beautiful.

MARK: I don't know what to…

CLAUDE: But you really do have to have the big money in this world. You understand? A man has to be rich or life is just like a…like a big shit.
(*MARK now sinks down to his knees and holds onto CLAUDE's legs.*)

MARK: Thank you so much. Thank you so…so much. I can't believe it. I really can't believe it.

CLAUDE: Please…stand up.
(*MARK continues.*)
What are you doing?
(*From the hall exit we hear the flashing and whirring of many cameras.*)

VOICES: Caroline, Caroline…if we could have one of the both of you. Just a few more, love. If you could ask Claude to come out just one more time etc…
(*We hear a door slam off.*
MARK continues his drunken homage to the embarrassed CLAUDE.
CAROLINE, in her coat, comes through into the kitchen and then out onto the terrace. She stops in her tracks when she sees MARK still bowing and scraping to CLAUDE, hands around the man's ankles.)

MARK: My problems are… I mean, I don't know what to… I'm just so… Thank you, Claude. You've saved me, saved me… You've really gone and saved my life.
(*MARK now starts sobbing at CLAUDE's feet.*)
You're a beautiful man, such a beautiful, beautiful man…
(*CLAUDE and CAROLINE watch him.*)
You've saved me.

CLAUDE: It's okay.

MARK: I love you for this. I just love you for this, Claude. For the rest of my life, for the rest of my days, I love you, I love you. I love you…

CAROLINE: What a touching scene.
(*MARK turns round. Embarrassed, he then struggles to his feet.*)
There are easily twenty photographers outside now.

CLAUDE: This happens, baby.

CAROLINE: How on earth do you propose we escape?

CLAUDE: We wait.

CAROLINE: I assure you that is simply not an option.

MARK: (*To CLAUDE.*) Good luck with it.
(*MARK now comes past CAROLINE. He pats her on the arm with drunken sympathy. He enters the kitchen, where LINDSAY still sits, dejected. He slowly walks towards the table, and stands behind her, swaying a little. She looks at him briefly, then looks away.*)

CAROLINE: What's he talking about?

CLAUDE: Caroline, there is something I must say to you. It is…not so easy for me…

CAROLINE: You *are* looking rather severe.

CLAUDE: I have been thinking since the last two weeks or so that…you and I…well, it is maybe time for us to… (*He breaks off.*) *C'est très difficile.*

CAROLINE: Oh my God, I can't believe it!

CLAUDE: It is time for us to…

CAROLINE: The answer's yes! The answer is of course a resounding YES!

CLAUDE: I do not…

(*CAROLINE walks towards him and embraces the stunned man.*)

CAROLINE: But why ask me at this ghastly little event? Why on earth couldn't you have waited until later on tonight? (*They kiss, he reluctantly, bewildered.*)

SCENE 2

On the terrace. It is darker. RUTH is seated at the table, staring sadly into space. STEVE stands protectively behind her. CLAUDE and CAROLINE stand to one side, hand in hand.

CAROLINE: As I say, I did think he was up to something.

STEVE: Congratulations then.

CLAUDE: Listen…

CAROLINE: I simply can't wait to tell everybody.

CLAUDE: We must talk…

CAROLINE: We can discuss all the fine details later.

CLAUDE: Listen…

CAROLINE: Do you think we should announce it to the press now?

CLAUDE: But you are not listening…

CAROLINE: I have to be honest with you, I never really saw myself as the marrying kind. It just always seemed like such an unnecessary restriction of one's precious freedoms but I suppose it turns out I'm quite an idealist after all, doesn't it? A hopeless romantic.

STEVE: I hope you'll be very happy.

CLAUDE: We must talk…

CAROLINE: And you're married, are you?

STEVE: I was.

CAROLINE: And it didn't work out for you?

STEVE: I was very young and we...

CAROLINE: You see, sometimes you just know when something's right, don't you?

STEVE: I suffered from...

CAROLINE: It's only since I've met this young man here... that I've realised that maybe, yes...I've been missing out on something after all.

STEVE: ...depression.

CAROLINE: When I'm away from him – and of course, doing what we both do, we have to spend far too much time apart – when I'm away from him, I've started to feel... just a little bit...lost at sea. And when I'm with him, when I'm looking into his eyes and hearing this voice of his... I just feel that I'm...home. That I've finally come home. Do you know what I'm talking about? I really can't wait to tell everyone.

I suddenly feel so very...happy.

CLAUDE: We must talk.

CAROLINE: Can't it wait?

CLAUDE: No. Please.

(*He brings her forward.*)

CAROLINE: Why don't we give those wretched men outside the photographs they're after and then we just can go?

CLAUDE: Caroline...

CAROLINE: Because if we don't they'll just be following us to the hotel.

CLAUDE: You must listen.

CAROLINE: And they'll completely ruin our weekend.

CLAUDE: Do you hear?

CAROLINE: I'm so happy, Claude. I really can't believe this.

(*To RUTH.*) Is everything alright, over there?

(*RUTH is now very drunk and in a world of her own.*)

(*To STEVE.*) Is she alright?

RUTH: Where are the others?

STEVE: Upstairs.

RUTH: I'm ready now.

STEVE: What for?

CAROLINE: Is this surprise going to take very long?

RUTH: (*Slurring.*) A little surprise.

CAROLINE: I'm sorry?

RUTH: Surprise. Ready.

CAROLINE: Well, we're all on tenterhooks I can assure you.

(*Now LINDSAY, upset, comes into the kitchen from the hall.*)

LINDSAY: Just leave me alone.

(*MARK now follows her into the kitchen.*
It is clear that the company outside can hear the following
exchange. They listen in an embarrassed silence.)

MARK: I just want you to listen to me.

LINDSAY: I'm not interested.

MARK: I said I was sorry.

LINDSAY: It's too late.

MARK: I won't do it again.

LINDSAY: I've had enough, Mark.

MARK: I'll make it up to you.

LINDSAY: I want you to move out.

MARK: You what?

LINDSAY: I want you to…go. I need some time on my own.

MARK: What are you talking about?

LINDSAY: It's just not working.

MARK: What's not?

LINDSAY: You and me. The whole thing.

MARK: But you're my… I'm your…

LINDSAY: You're unhappy, I'm unhappy.

MARK: It's going to change.

LINDSAY: I think you should stay with your brother. Just for a
time.

MARK: Listen to me.

LINDSAY: I need to get my head straight.

MARK: Look, I know I've had a drink tonight… I know I have.
I'm an idiot. But I have been trying.

LINDSAY: I don't want to talk about it here.

MARK: You can't leave me.

LINDSAY: Just for a few months. See how it goes.

MARK: What about the kids?

LINDSAY: We'll manage.

MARK: I need to see my kids.

LINDSAY: You can see them. I just don't want you in the house any more. I'm sorry.

MARK: And this is all because of the horse?

LINDSAY: (*After a pause.*) Of course not.

MARK: Because I said we couldn't afford this horse?

LINDSAY: It's not just the horse, Mark. We have to get her into that school. You said we could get her into the school.

MARK: I've worked so hard. To give you the house, give you the holidays. Grafted all my life.

LINDSAY: I know you have.

MARK: And all because of some stupid…

LINDSAY: It's not just that. It's your drinking, it's your moods…

MARK: I've stopped drinking.

LINDSAY: Mark, you can hardly stand up.

MARK: I'm not drunk.

(*He leans on the back of a chair and pulls it over.*)

LINDSAY: You need therapy.

MARK: Don't start that.

LINDSAY: I can recommend someone.

MARK: Where will I stay?

LINDSAY: And to be honest: I don't love you any more.

(*MARK holds onto the table for support, stunned.*)

I'm sorry.

(*She turns to go outside.*)

MARK: You got me wrong.

LINDSAY: I'm going.

MARK: There's something you should know.

LINDSAY: Did you hear?

MARK: Been saving.

LINDSAY: (*Turning.*) I'm sorry?

MARK: For a while. Been saving hard.

LINDSAY: I don't know what you mean.

MARK: I wanted it to be a surprise. For both of you.

LINDSAY: You've been saving? For what?

MARK: For the…for the…horse.

(*A silence.*)

Been saving hard. We can get it next week. So…
(*He faces her, swaying.*)
Give me another chance. Please. I'll make it up to you.
I'll try harder. I'll do anything. Anything. I'll make it right
again. You know I'll make it right again. You'll love me
again. Please say you'll love me again.

LINDSAY: I don't want to discuss it here.

MARK: (*Taking out his car keys.*) Then lets go home.

LINDSAY: Give me those.

MARK: Oh, I'm alright.

LINDSAY: You are drunk, Mark. Give me those.

MARK: I'm fine, honestly. It'll be fine.

LINDSAY: I'll count to three.

MARK: Then you drive.

LINDSAY: I'm drunk.

MARK: No, you're not.

LINDSAY: Yes, I am.

MARK: No, you're not.

LINDSAY: I'm completely drunk.

MARK: You look alright to me.

LINDSAY: That's because you're drunk.

MARK: No, I'm not.

LINDSAY: Of course you are.

MARK: Oh, come on…

LINDSAY: Give!
(*MARK tosses her the keys. They then stare at each other for a
time, both pissed, both lost.*)

MARK: I love you, Lindse. (*Tearful.*) I love you so much.

LINDSAY: (*After a pause.*) I know you do, Mark. I know you do.
(*She looks at him for a time, perhaps won over, and then turns
and walks out. She is met by yet another embarrassed silence.*)
(*Cheerfully.*) Lovely evening now, isn't it?
(*He follows her onto the terrace.
RUTH now slowly and drunkenly stands. She is very drunk and
very distraught, out of control.*)
So…Ruth…it's been really nice. Really very…nice. (*A pause.*)
Hasn't it, Mark?

MARK: Sorry?

LINDSAY: Hasn't it been nice?

MARK: Yeah. Sorry. It's been really nice. (*A pause.*) Thank you.

LINDSAY: Yes. Thank you.

MARK: Really nice.

LINDSAY: Yes.

MARK: Really good.

LINDSAY: Really nice to...see...everyone.

> (*A long silence.*)
> So...Ruth...bit embarrassing actually but we're both a bit over the limit actually so we were wondering if you might possibly be able to recommend a...

RUTH: This is it. This is it for me. The end of the road. Here. Now. You understand me?

CAROLINE: What are you talking about?

RUTH: Have you any idea...have any of you any idea what it's like to be this alone? To be so lonely that you can't even think. So lonely you can't even breathe. Most days I just wonder around the house. Don't know what to do with myself...just don't know what to do. And you know outside your window it's all going on without you and the world's this great party and you're not invited to it. You're too dull, you're too...dull, dull, dull. And so I've invited you to *my* party, since you wouldn't invite me to *yours.* This is *my* party, *my* party...my...

CAROLINE: I don't mean to be insensitive but...

RUTH: Not another word from you!

CAROLINE: I beg your pardon?

RUTH: You've said enough.

STEVE: Ruth...

RUTH: (*To STEVE.*) And you please...just go.

STEVE: Come down.

CAROLINE: I think it's most definitely time to go now.

> (*CAROLINE makes a move to go.*)

RUTH: I want you two to know... All those years. How you made me feel. Both of you. So mean, so cruel. (*She points her finger at CAROLINE.*) You...the things you used to say.

CAROLINE: I don't know what you're talking about.

> (*RUTH now turns and points her finger at LINDSAY.*)

RUTH: And I thought you were my friend.

LINDSAY: I was…

RUTH: But you put me down, you put me down…

LINDSAY: Then I'm sorry.

> (*She points her finger at CAROLINE.*)

RUTH: You! You called me Blubberbelly.

> (*MARK lets out a snort of laughter. Over the next section he tries to keep hold of himself but his hysterical laughter eventually spirals out of control.*)

CAROLINE: I don't remember…

RUTH: (*To LINDSAY.*) And *you* called me Blubberbelly.

LINDSAY: I'm so sorry.

RUTH: Blubberbelly. Whale Woman. Wobblebottom.

> (*A long silence. RUTH dangerously sways on the table.*)

LINDSAY: (*Fighting back tears.*) I'm so sorry…

RUTH: The reason I ate… The reason I…

STEVE: Ruth, please…

RUTH: My sister, she… When she was only a baby… It ate her up. From the inside. And then we…

STEVE: (*To the others.*) I think you should all just leave now.

RUTH: (*Breaking.*) My mother, she… Couldn't… She stopped living, 'Why didn't *you* die, Ruth? Why wasn't it *you*?'

> (*MARK eventually gains controls himself. A silence.*)

CAROLINE: Then we're sorry.

RUTH: You're…?

LINDSAY: I'm so sorry.

CAROLINE: We were only children.

RUTH: That day. In the pool. And you both laughed. You laughed at my disgusting body. You pulled off my costume. Stripped me down. Stripped me naked. She dared you and you did it. To be her friend. You stripped me naked and I begged you and you laughed…

LINDSAY: (*All coming back to her.*) Oh my God…

RUTH: You laughed and you laughed and you laughed…

LINDSAY: (*Upset.*) Please…

RUTH: Ran off with it. Threw it up into a tree.

LINDSAY: Oh God…

RUTH: And you left me there and then my sister died and you left me there and I stayed in the water until the caretaker found me and threw me out I was so ashamed and he got me a towel and then my sister died and I went home and I cried and I cried and I…

STEVE: Ruth…

RUTH: Never get into the swing of things. Some people. Not good at anything. We just…fail. Nothing works. Nobody notices. And we fail. We just…fail.

(*Nobody speaks as she sobs.*)

CLAUDE: I have listened to you with great care, Ruth, and I must now reassure you that…

RUTH: (*Suddenly angry.*) And don't you talk to me about God and nature! There is no God, you idiots! Of course there's no God! It's all just animals and plants eating each other and fighting and raping and eating each other. I've seen it! Ugly, brutal. Savage. No beauty, no beauty, no beauty in any of it!

(*She now breaks completely.*)

What kind of God gives a child cancer? You idiots! We're all in this alone!

(*STEVE holds out his hand to her.*)

On our own, on our own, on our own…

(*She sobs terribly.*

STEVE approaches her, tentatively. He is unsure what to say to her as she sobs. He keeps trying to speak but cannot. Meanwhile: LINDSAY, very upset, rushes out and heads for the kitchen area. She covers her face with a hand.)

CAROLINE: (*To CLAUDE.*) This was all years ago.

CLAUDE: It is finished.

CAROLINE: And she's inventing parts of it.

CLAUDE: I do not want we see each other again.

CAROLINE: I'm sorry?

CLAUDE: I do not want to see you any more.

(*MARK is about to follow his wife into the kitchen. CLAUDE clicks his fingers.*)

We are ready for you over here, Mr Mark.

CAROLINE: (*Stunned.*) But all this happened...such a...long time...ago.

CLAUDE: I'm very sorry.

CAROLINE: We...were only...children.

CAROLINE: I go now.

(*As CLAUDE turns to go, CAROLINE grabs hold of his arm.*)

CLAUDE: Let go of me!

CAROLINE: I won't let you do this!

CLAUDE: Please...take your hand off me!

CAROLINE: But I love you!

CLAUDE: I ask you one more time!

CAROLINE: Please, no...

CLAUDE: I will become quite angry.

CAROLINE: But you don't understand...you are my last chance! My last chance at happiness...

(*He flings her off him and she crashes desolate to the ground. MARK now makes another move towards the kitchen but CLAUDE claps a hand on his shoulder.*)

CLAUDE: Okay, Mr Mark...you now earn your money, yes? You take the lady where she needs to go.

(*CLAUDE goes through into the kitchen. He looks at the upset LINDSAY for a time and then goes out.*
We hear knocking on the offstage door.)

VOICES: Claude! Claude! Open up, mate! Be a sport!!

(*On the terrace, torn between consoling his wife and CAROLINE, he approaches the prostrate woman.*)

MARK: Is everything alright over here?

(*CAROLINE moans terribly.*)

You want a cup of tea or...?

CAROLINE: (*Screaming through her tears.*) Why don't you just go to hell, you appalling little man!

(*CLAUDE now comes back into the kitchen, putting on his jacket. He approaches LINDSAY.*)

CLAUDE: These people. They are crazy. But you and me, we do not belong here. So if you ever want to come party with Claude Kabinda, then my number goes in your pocket right now...

(*He slips a piece of paper into the back pocket of her trousers. As he does so she screams.*)

LINDSAY: Go away, go away, go away!!!

(*MARK now grabs a garden fork that's lying close at hand. He rushes into the kitchen. He sees CLAUDE standing close behind LINDSAY. He jabs the fork towards CLAUDE.*)

MARK: That's my wife! My wife! You understand? Get away from her! You just get right away from her!

CLAUDE: Easy, Mr Mark! Easy now…

(*Torn between the two unfolding crises STEVE runs after MARK into the kitchen, as RUTH continues to sob on the table outside.*)

MARK: That's my wife!! You got your own. You got any woman you want! You're Claude Kabinda! But you leave mine alone. She belongs to me and I'll put this through you! I'll put this right through your stinking black heart.

CLAUDE: That is not such a nice thing to say, Mr Mark.

MARK: She's my woman, my woman, yes?!

STEVE: Put that down, Mark.

MARK: Nothing to do with you!

CLAUDE: He make me laugh.

MARK: Get away from my wife.

STEVE: Drop your weapon now, please.

MARK: (*Turning and swinging at STEVE.*) You going to make me?

STEVE: I am, yes.

MARK: I'll knock your head off.

STEVE: And I'll break both your arms before you even move.

CLAUDE: (*To LINDSAY.*) You really want to throw your life away on a loser like this?

MARK: (*Turning back.*) What you say?

CLAUDE: In life, baby, there are winners, yes…there and winners and there are losers and…

LINDSAY: Mark, don't…

MARK: What did you call me?

(*He spits on the ground near MARK's feet and then walks back to the hall in contempt.*
A silence.)

LINDSAY: Mark, don't…

(*MARK now bellows with a terrible rage and charges off after him.*
STEVE follows.
A crash. A silence.
We then hear CLAUDE's painful screaming off.
CAROLINE hears this and also rushes through into the kitchen.)

CAROLINE: Claude! Claude? What have they done to my baby?

(*As all this is happening, RUTH recovers and sees she is alone. She then slowly walks to the back of the terrace area and produces a length of rope. She returns to the table, steps onto it, via the chair, and starts to tie one end of the rope to the branch of the overhanging tree.*)

CLAUDE: (*Off.*) *Ma carrière! Ma carrière! Une ambulance, une ambulance!!*

(*STEVE now carries CLAUDE into the kitchen.*
CLAUDE's right foot is bleeding heavily.)
Une ambulance! Une ambulance!
(*MARK now comes in, holding the fork.*)
(*Screaming.*) You will pay for this!! You will pay! I will make you pay! You think I buy your horse now, uh! You think I help with your gamble debts!? Not now! Not now!
(*He spits at MARK.*
LINDSAY looks at her husband.)

STEVE: (*On his phone.*) Yes, please. As quick as you can.

CLAUDE: Now Claude Kabinda, he ruin you! Claude Kabinda, he ruin you! He take away all the pennies that you have!!
(*STEVE now lies CLAUDE on the kitchen table. He holds CLAUDE's bleeding foot up and then gives it to LINDSAY to hold.*)
(*To MARK.*) May God strike you down for what you have done! May God strike you down!

LINDSAY: (*To MARK.*) What gambling debts?
(*LINDSAY and MARK regard each other in horror as CLAUDE writhes in agony.*
STEVE wraps some tea towels around CLAUDE's foot.)

CAROLINE: Claude, I love you! Please. I can't live without you…

CLAUDE: Now Claude Kabinda ruin you! Claude Kabinda, he ruin you!

LINDSAY: (*To MARK.*) What debts, Mark?

(*More hammering on the offstage door. It continues.*)

VOICES: Come on, Claude! Just one of you and the lovely Caroline. Just one of the happy couple and then we're done!

(*STEVE now rushes out onto the terrace where he is confronted by the sight of RUTH now standing on the table, the noose around her neck.*)

STEVE: Jesus Christ!

RUTH: Please…just go.

(*She seems about to kick the table away.*)

STEVE: (*Very urgent.*) Wait! Listen to me, listen! Please. I've spent the money. From the book. The advance and…I bought this boat. Small one. Doing it up. Sold everything and I got this boat. Going to go up every river in the country. For a year. Maybe two. Until the cash runs out. Maybe write something else. Get into the country, get under the sky. So…come with me. We're good mates, you and me. On the same wavelength, Ruth. You're not on your own, you know. Not unless you want to be. You'll be restored. Really. We'll get out there into all that green. It's all we need. Wake up every morning to the sound of the birds and the water against the boat and we'll go down the rivers slowly, slowly. Ever so slowly. We'll go down the rivers with nowhere to go, with nothing to do, with nothing to say even. Forget about the world, forget about the…people, the work, the whole lot of it. We'll just…be. And…we'll be free, Ruth. Just you and me. Believe me. We really will be…we really will be completely…completely free.

(*She looks at him with a profound sadness. She then smiles. It seems she's about to rethink. Then, suddenly, she kicks over the table. Almost immediately the branch breaks with a loud crack and she hits the ground hard.*

*In the kitchen, it is madness, chaos: CLAUDE moaning in agony
on the table, CAROLINE in shock, LINDSAY staring at MARK in
disbelief, while holding CLAUDE's foot up. Hammering on the
door. The flashlights of the cameras.*
Soon the sound of a distant ambulance siren.)

RUTH: (*Sobbing.*) I'm so useless. I really can't do anything.
I can't do anything at all. Oh, all I want to do is disappear.
God knows… God knows all I wanted to do was disappear.
(*Soon the lights fade in the kitchen just as the sounds and the
chaos recede.*
*On the terrace we now hear birdsong and the sound of water
gently lapping against the hull of a boat. STEVE approaches
the prostrate woman. He holds out a hand to her. She looks at
him. After a time she raises her hand and then it moves slowly
towards his.*)

THE COMPANY MAN

Characters

JANE
60s (and 40s), a dying woman

WILLIAM
60s (and 40s), her husband

JIM
60s (and 40s), their friend

RICHARD
mid-late 30s, their son

CATHY
early 30s, their daughter

This is a very wealthy household somewhere in Southern England's commuter belt. Three playing areas: the terrace, the living room, a bedroom.

The action takes place over one weekend in summer and over various periods twenty years previously.

Act One

SCENE 1

Music as introduction is Bach's Prelude No 1 in C Major, from the 'Well-Tempered Clavier Book 1' – or something similar. It's played from an old scratched LP. Friday. Close to midnight.

A shaft of moonlight across the terrace. After a time we see the headlights of a car and hear the crunch of tyres over gravel. We hear a car door opening and then closing. RICHARD comes onto the terrace with a large shoulder bag. After a time a light goes on in the house. CATHY comes into the living room. She then appears on the terrace. The music fades.

CATHY: (*In an undertone.*) We've been expecting you all day.
   (*No response.*)
   You were supposed to be here for lunch.
   (*After a time RICHARD goes to her. He initiates an embrace. A long silence as RICHARD does not disengage.*)
   What's the matter? Where's Thongbai?
   (*No response.*)
   Where's Jack?

RICHARD: Not coming.

CATHY: (*Disengaging.*) Why not? You know how much Mum…

RICHARD: I'll ask her…next week… I'll make sure she brings him…

CATHY: You don't understand…

RICHARD: I'm sorry…

CATHY: So, what's happened?
   (*No response.*)
   Are you two…?

RICHARD: How are thing here?

CATHY: Things are exhausting. Things are…sad.
   (*A long silence.*)

RICHARD: It's good to see you.

CATHY: (*A pause.*) It's good to see you.

RICHARD: How long you going to stay here?

CATHY: As long as it takes.

RICHARD: And how long's that going to be?

CATHY: (*After a pause.*) Not long.

RICHARD: And then it's off to Africa?

CATHY: And then it's off to Africa.
 (*A silence.*)
RICHARD: How is she?
CATHY: She gets very depressed.
RICHARD: Don't blame her.
CATHY: And scared.
RICHARD: She's not the only one.
CATHY: What are you scared of?
RICHARD: Living. Scares me to death.
 (*A long silence.*)
 Listen, I hate to ask you but…you couldn't see your way
 clear to lending me a…
CATHY: I've told you before, Richard, so please understand…
 I'm earning nothing at the moment. I look after Mum. I
 have no money at all.
 (*Neither speak.*)
RICHARD: It's a beautiful night.
CATHY: Yes.
RICHARD: Full moon. Stars.
CATHY: Are you and her… I mean, are you…?
RICHARD: It's not your problem.
CATHY: Of course it's my problem…
RICHARD: It's my life.
CATHY: Someone's got to keep this family together…
RICHARD: Why's that then?
CATHY: And Dad's going to need all the family around him
 that…
RICHARD: (*A sudden rage.*) Dad can go and fuck himself!
 (*Twelve slow chimes from the nearby church.*
 She looks up at the sky again. So does he.)
CATHY: He was showing me his new telescope this evening.
 Introducing me to the wonders of astronomy. It's amazing
 actually. Every star perfectly in its place. He's developing
 quite a passion for it.
 (*Neither speak.*)
 She was so looking forward to seeing that little boy.
RICHARD: Next week.
CATHY: Next week's no good.

(*A silence.*)

RICHARD: Anyway, thanks for…doing the honours here.

CATHY: I'm a trained nurse, Richard. You work at a wine warehouse.

(*RICHARD walks to the table. He sits. A long silence.*)

RICHARD: Something's happened.

CATHY: Tell me.

RICHARD: Something bad has happened.

CATHY: So tell me.

(*A long silence.*
He then kicks out one of the chairs towards her.
CATHY looks at it, walks over towards it and sits.
Neither speak for a time.)

RICHARD: I've made a mess of my life.

CATHY: We know.

(*RICHARD now opens his bag, takes out a half-drunk bottle of wine and a glass.*)

What's that?

RICHARD: What does it look like?

CATHY: What are you doing?

RICHARD: Having a drink.

CATHY: Since when?

RICHARD: Since about a month ago.

CATHY: I don't believe this.

RICHARD: Listen, can we please just talk…?

CATHY: (*Standing.*) What are you thinking of?

RICHARD: I'll give it up again when things…

(*She makes a sudden grab for the bottle but he gets there first.*
Inside, a light goes on.
CATHY turns on her heels and marches back into the house. As she does so she encounters her father, WILLIAM, in his pyjamas and dressing gown, in the living room.
Outside on the terrace, RICHARD pours himself a drink. He wanders around the terrace, deep in thought.)

WILLIAM: What are you doing up?

CATHY: Nothing.

WILLIAM: I thought I heard voices.

CATHY: Richard's here.

WILLIAM: Oh, that's smashing.

CATHY: I'd leave it until the morning, if I were…

WILLIAM: Two years, three months and sixteen days.

CATHY: Sorry?

WILLIAM: Since he's been here. Two years, three months and sixteen days.

CATHY: I see.

WILLIAM: I looked it up.

CATHY: Well, Dad, you… You just go back to…

WILLIAM: Is your mother alright?

CATHY: She was asleep just now so…

WILLIAM: She doesn't deserve all this, you know.

CATHY: No…

WILLIAM: She's a good girl, that one. A real good old girl. (*A pause.*) A love.

(*A silence.*)

Might just pop out and say hello.

CATHY: Dad, listen…

WILLIAM: Nice to have you both here again, isn't it? You know how long it's been? Since we were all here together? All four of us?

CATHY: A long time.

WILLIAM: It's been a very long time. (*A pause.*) Do you have any idea?

CATHY: I don't, no…

WILLIAM: Twenty-one years.

CATHY: Really?

WILLIAM: Since we were all here together.

CATHY: Twenty-one years?

WILLIAM: Twenty-one years. Twenty-one Christmases. (*A pause.*) I looked it up.

CATHY: Anyway, I'm going to see how Mum's doing and then…

WILLIAM: It's a very long time, is that.

(*CATHY makes to go.*)

(*To himself.*) Lot of water. Under the…bridge.

CATHY: (*Turning.*) Sorry?

WILLIAM: Do you like my sunflowers then?

CATHY: I do. They're…

WILLIAM: Pretty impressive, would you not say?

CATHY: They're beautiful, Dad. As always they're…

WILLIAM: As tall as you like.

CATHY: You had a good day out there, didn't you?

WILLIAM: Really opening up now. (*A pause.*) I had a really good day today. A really good old day.

(*CATHY exits.*

WILLIAM looks off at RICHARD on the terrace.)

(*To himself.*) My…little man.

(*WILLIAM now comes out onto the terrace. Unobserved he watches his son.*

RICHARD knocks back another glass.)

Two years, three months and sixteen days.

RICHARD: (*Turning, startled.*) Sorry?

WILLIAM: Two years, three months and sixteen days. Since you've been here.

RICHARD: That long, is it?

WILLIAM: I looked it up.

(*A long silence. WILLIAM walks towards RICHARD. They stand close to each other. Tentatively WILLIAM holds out a hand to his son. It's not taken. A long silence.*)

Having a…having a good old drink, are you?

RICHARD: I am.

WILLIAM: Don't mind me. (*After a pause.*) It's your liver.

(*A silence.*)

(*Inside, a bedside light goes on in the bedroom and we see CATHY at the side of a bed, in which sleeps her mother, JANE. She checks on her. Back outside:*)

So…any news then?

RICHARD: Sorry?

WILLIAM: Anything to report?

RICHARD: Not really.

WILLIAM: Still assistant manager?

RICHARD: Still assistant manager.

WILLIAM: Well, that's good then. To be assistant. Isn't it? The world needs its assistants. Only a matter of time…

(*A silence.*)

Anyway. Yes. That's all good then.

(*A silence.*)

So where's that grandson of mine then?

RICHARD: Coming tomorrow.

WILLIAM: Oh, he's coming tomorrow, is he? That'll be nice
then.

(*A silence.*)

And how's that lovely Thai bride of yours…?

RICHARD: She's fine.

(*A silence.*

Inside JANE coughs painfully.)

WILLIAM: I was going to get a…get a little something for the
lad but…well, as I say, I saw something in the shop but…

RICHARD: Forget it.

WILLIAM: Didn't know whether it would be quite suitable
so I…

RICHARD: It's the thought, isn't it?

WILLIAM: I wasn't quite sure whether…

(*In the bedroom.*)

CATHY: Didn't mean to wake you.

JANE: Could I have some water, please?

(*JANE suffers from motor neurone disease and this affects her
speech. It is comprehensible yet a little laboured.*

CATHY pours her a glass of water.

Outside:)

WILLIAM: So…the lad's well then?

RICHARD: (*After a pause.*) Like I say, he's fine.

WILLIAM: That's good.

(*In the bedroom.*)

JANE: Where does all the time go to?

CATHY: I don't know.

JANE: Don't waste your precious time. I've wasted so much of
my time. So much time, so much precious, precious time…

(*CATHY opens a bedside drawer, while outside:*)

WILLIAM: And so…how's things? How's…work?

RICHARD: Dull and depressing.

(*In the bedroom.*)

JANE: I hope I've not been an awful mother to you.

CATHY: (*After a pause.*) You haven't.

JANE: Because I do have regrets.

CATHY: You're to regret nothing.

JANE: I just want to go with a clean slate. I don't want any resentment.

CATHY: Mum…

JANE: I want to apologise for anything I've done to upset anyone…but I do realise that…your father and I… I know it's not always been an especially happy home…

CATHY: Forget about the past.

JANE: But, you see, that's such a hard thing to do.

(*Outside:*)

WILLIAM: Well, anyway, it's really good to see you again. Really is…

(*A silence.*)

I'm glad that things are…working out for you. Finally.

(*A silence.*)

What I mean is…you've got your lovely wife now, haven't you, and your boy and your good old bricks and mortar…

(*A pause.*) Just as long as you're happier now. That's the main thing. I'm just glad I could help you out with it all.

(*In the bedroom:*)

JANE: I so need to see Jim again.

CATHY: He said he'll be here in the…

JANE: I do really feel the need to…feel the need to…

(*Outside:*)

WILLIAM: 'Bricks and mortar, bricks and mortar'. That's what your grandfather always used to say. 'You've nothing in this life if you've no bricks and mortar.' (*A pause.*) I thought maybe tomorrow we could have a game of chess? Be like the good old days?

RICHARD: Maybe.

(*A silence.*)

WILLIAM: And you'll have to have a look round the garden. I've grown these sunflowers.

RICHARD: Oh yes?

WILLIAM: They're as tall as you like.

(*In the bedroom:*)

JANE: He was always such a…

CATHY: Listen, you sleep now.

JANE: Was my…absolute…my absolute…

CATHY: I'll just do your…

JANE: And I've missed him so very much.

(*CATHY now helps her mother move forward in the bed and she adjusts the pillows, while outside:*)

WILLIAM: I was talking to Harry Morris this week. Which of his sons was in your year? (*A slight laugh.*) Morris major or Morris minor?

RICHARD: I don't remember…

WILLIAM: I was sure the older brother was in your year?

(*No response.*)

Anyway, they're both doing very well. One's a top diplomat over in Germany somewhere and the other's an international lawyer.

(*In the bedroom CATHY is preparing some medication for her mother.*)

CATHY: This'll help you back to sleep.

JANE: I've been thinking a lot about him. Jim. Been having these dreams. So kind, so attentive. All those years when you were both small. He drove me to the hospital, I gave birth to you with him by my side and then he brought us both back again. (*A pause.*) Your father was too busy. (*Outside:*)

WILLIAM: Both of them on six-figure… (*He breaks off. A pause.*) Well, listen. Thanks for coming. I think your mother…

RICHARD: You don't need to thank me.

WILLIAM: I don't want to be… But if I'm to be perfectly honest, I think it's rather broken your mother's heart that you've not really…

RICHARD: (*Making a move.*) Right. I'm in my old room, I assume?

(*In the bedroom:*)

JANE: I'm terribly worried about him. I don't know how he's going to manage after…

CATHY: Don't think about it now.

JANE: He can't do anything for himself. He can't even boil an egg. He won't pay for a cleaner or a gardener.

CATHY: I'll talk to him.

JANE: No-one comes to visit him. He doesn't see anyone any more. Nobody from the company bothers with him now. Every day for forty-five years working for that company but you wouldn't know it. Forty-five years and he's not got one friend from all that time. And why is that? He kept that firm running so well. He kept them all in jobs and pensions and the profits were always so…

CATHY: I think people were probably intimidated by him, weren't they?

JANE: Oh, I don't believe that…

(*Outside:*)

WILLIAM: I hope I haven't offended you?

RICHARD: You haven't.

(*RICHARD, having put his bottle inside, picks up the shoulder bag and carries it into the house and off.*

WILLIAM watches him. Alone, he now looks up at the starlit sky.)

WILLIAM: All be over one day anyway. In a big, beautiful, blinding flash of light. All be over one fine day.

(*In the bedroom:*)

JANE: He's going to be so lonely, you see.

CATHY: Here.

(*CATHY now gives her mother the medication and helps her drink some water.*)

JANE: Loneliness, Cathy. At your father's age. It really is a terrible thing.

CATHY: Come on now…

JANE: To live alone day after day and without love. Without… touch. It's an absolutely awful thing.

CATHY: Mum…

JANE: Just you wait and see.

(*She settles back into her bed.*

CATHY helps make her comfortable. She then kisses her mother and turns off the light.

Outside on the terrace WILLIAM looks sadly about him. He then notices the glass that RICHARD was drinking from. He picks it up. Smells it. The smell sickens him, he grimaces and then puts the glass down again.)

SCENE 2

A light change. Twenty years earlier. Day. JANE sits on the sofa, head in hands, in despair. JIM stands behind her. He is uncertain as to how to comfort her. Then, outside, we hear a car screech to a sudden halt on the gravel.

JANE: Drunk in class.

JIM: He can easily finish his education somewhere else.

JANE: Drunk in class and he hits a teacher.

(*We hear the car door slamming.*)

He's had to cancel a meeting and he just gets so furious.

JIM: Then we'll have to try our best to...

JANE: He's only ever wanted what's best for him though. He's only ever wanted him to have the best possible start. He had such an awful childhood. I know he's too hard sometimes but he just wants the boy to have a good life.

JIM: I know this.

JANE: He means it all for the best.

(*In a fury, WILLIAM storms in, wearing a suit. His demeanour is utterly different from the rather uncertain and self-apologetic character of the previous scene.*)

WILLIAM: Where is he?

JANE: In your office.

WILLIAM: This time he's gone too far!

JANE: Don't be too hard on him.

WILLIAM: Get off me please!

JANE: He's very upset.

WILLIAM: They've expelled him, you say?!

JANE: On the spot.

WILLIAM: I'll have a word with the Head.

JANE: There's no point. They won't listen to...

WILLIAM: Of course they will, I'm on the board of bloody governors!

JANE: You don't understand, he's punched a...

(*WILLIAM exits.*
We hear muffled voices off.
JANE makes to follow her husband.)

JIM: Leave him.

JANE: But you don't know… You just don't know… This is all my fault.

JIM: Of course it's not your…

JANE: I should have intervened years ago…

WILLIAM: (*Shouting, off.*) And you can bloody well wipe that smirk off your face when I'm talking to you!!

JANE: His father was a drunken bully and…

JIM: We know all this….

JANE: They had no money at all, and so all he wants…

JIM: He just wants what's best.

JANE: He only wants what's best.

WILLIAM: (*Shouting, off.*) And are you drunk? Have you been drinking?

JANE: I really don't know where we've gone wrong with him.

JIM: He's a good, bright boy. He's just rebelling against…

JANE: But he is so contrary. God knows what's going to become of him…

WILLIAM: (*Shouting, off.*) Well, do you have you any idea how much it's cost me to put you through this 'stupid fucking school', as you so eloquently describe it?!
Do you?! Do you, boy!?

JANE: It's the one thing that sets him off. The thought that his son is wasting his life. That's not such a bad thing to care about, is it? It's not so bad to want what's best for him?

JIM: Of course not.

RICHARD: (*Shouting, off.*) Don't come near me with that! Don't you come anywhere near me with…

(*A loud crash off as the men fall onto a desk or a bookshelf. We then hear a door slam.*
WILLIAM now comes back into the living room, head tilted back, cupping his bleeding nose in one hand. He shouts after his son.)

I want you out of this house! You hear me? I want him out, Jane. He pushed me. Pushed me right over! You're a waste of space, boy! A waste of bloody space! This is my house and these are my rules. So I want him out, Jane! Right now! (*Calling off.*) You're on your own now, sunbeam. Oh yes, consider yourself well and truly on your own.

JANE: (*Making a move off.*) Richard!

WILLIAM: (*Preventing her.*) Leave him. Let him go. Let him go to hell!

JANE: We have to help him.

WILLIAM: He's had all the help he's going to get in this house. (*A moment of hesitation as JANE is caught between seeing to her husband and her son. She chooses WILLIAM and helps him onto the sofa.*) Lets just see how he survives now. In the world on his own with no qualifications. With no nothing. He won't last a second. Thinks he can blag his way through with his looks and his charm but he'll find out. He'll find out the hard way. He's not so bloody special, is he, and he'll find that out!

JANE: You've blood on your shirt.

WILLIAM: With that bloody synthesiser! Who does he think bought it for him? Thinks he can bring down the system, as he calls it, with a synthesiser! Well, I bought it for him, didn't I? I bought the bloody thing for him.

JANE: Just please calm down.

WILLIAM: And those awful cacophonous dirges he produces! (*She helps her husband off with his jacket and tie and then his blood-stained shirt.*) We've got a beautiful piano just there, look. A perfectly good piano from your parents. Lets hear some real music from him. Lets hear some Schubert, some Bach, some Beethoven, some bloody class, Jim!

JANE: Hold still…

WILLIAM: He's a waste of space, that one. Nothing more than a waste of bloody space!

JANE: Bill…

WILLIAM: You do well, Jim, I tell you. You do well not having children.

JIM: Bill, you've got two lovely…

WILLIAM: Oh, you've absolutely no idea what it's like, have you!

JANE: Come on, Bill…

WILLIAM: He's directionless, he's vague. He's got to work. I keep telling him. Apply yourself. Make a man of yourself. Make a choice. Be responsible. He's a dreamer. A bloody dreamer. Dreaming of getting the girls and the glory with his pretentious little pop band. But will he work for it? Will he hell. Doesn't know he's born! Oh for Christ's sake, I can't wear this shirt, can I? I'm the managing director, aren't I! How can the managing director be seen in a bloody shirt like this!

JANE: It's the only one that's ironed.

WILLIAM: Oh for crying out loud!

JANE: I'm sorry… I didn't imagine you were going to get blood…

WILLIAM: Where the hell did a shirt like that come from anyway?

JANE: I think your mother bought…

WILLIAM: Well, that useless cow was good for absolutely nothing, wasn't she?!

(*WILLIAM struggles into the clean shirt.*)

JANE: I'm sure if we talk to…

WILLIAM: Just a pathetic, simpering waste of space, wasn't she! Oh, this has shrunk in the wash, Jane. You must have shrunk it in the bloody wash!

JANE: I think you're just a little heavier, darling, than you were the last time you…

WILLIAM: No, there's no more to be said. That boy is no longer welcome in this house!

JIM: Bill, perhaps if we all…

WILLIAM: You keep out of this, Jim! It's got bugger all to do with you! And this shirt is a bloody joke… An absolute bloody joke.

(*WILLIAM storms out across the terrace and exiting:*)

It's just not good enough, is it! It's just bloody well not good enough!

(*A long silence in the living room.*)

JANE: You go home. This is not your problem.

JIM: I like to think I'm your friend.

JANE: Yes. You are. My God, but you are.

(*A silence for a time.*)

JIM: Come here, please.

JANE: I beg your pardon?

(*JIM now makes an uncertain move towards her and opens his arms.*)

What are you doing, sorry?

(*His arms go round her.*

WILLIAM, trying to calm himself, now reappears on the terrace. He paces about, rehearsing a speech in his head. As he walks towards the living room:)

WILLIAM: (*To himself.*) Okay so… I'm sorry, Jim… There was no call for… I'm really sorry about losing my…

(*Inside he stops in his tracks when he sees his wife in JIM's arms. He watches them unobserved for a time and then turns and goes back out.*)

JIM: You're not on your own, you know. In this life. I'd like to take this opportunity to reassure you of that.

(*We hear a car starting as off JANE breaks from the embrace slightly and looks up at JIM. They stare at each other for a time and then JIM tentatively attempts to kiss her. She pulls away. A moment of extreme awkwardness. They separate, she now with her back to him.*)

SCENE 3

The present. Saturday. A beautiful summer morning. Birdsong. In the bedroom, JANE turns in her bed. CATHY is seated close by, comforting her. WILLIAM comes onto the terrace from the garden. He has binoculars around his neck. He is writing in a notebook.

WILLIAM: (*To himself.*) The coal tit, Latin name: *parus ater*, times two. The jackdaw, Latin name: *corvus monedula*, times one. And the house sparrow, Latin name: *passer domesticus* times sixteen. Not on the decline in this part of the world are you, old friend? Not by a long stretch of the imagination. And what have we here? (*He brings the*

binoculars to his eyes.) I do believe it's a heron! Oh, beautiful, beautiful…
(*Behind him JIM comes on. He now walks with the aid of a stick.*)
The flight of the bird, the grace of the flight, it's a wonder of nature, it really is. Just glides slowly down…wings majestically open and then…stands still as a statue as if it's been stood at that spot all it's life. Oh, that's made my day. Better put that in my book, yes. I'll most definitely put that down in my little blue book.
(*He checks his watch, writes in his notebook.*)
9.18 am, grey heron, times one.

JIM: Hello, stranger…

WILLIAM: (*Turning.*) Jim!
(*A very long awkward silence.*)
Well…what can I say? It's been a long, long time…

JIM: It has.
(*A very long awkward silence.*)

WILLIAM: Don't know how you can live in stinking old London, Jim. Not when you've lived amongst all this greenery.

JIM: I needed a change of…

WILLIAM: Anyway, welcome back, welcome back…

JIM: I see you still love your birds then?

WILLIAM: The grey heron. You any idea what it's Latin name is?

JIM: I'm afraid not.

WILLIAM: *Ardea cinerea.* Isn't that a beautiful-sounding name?

JIM: Well, it certainly is a…

WILLIAM: *Ardea cinerea.* I think it's probably my favourite of all the birds.

JIM: Yes, well…they are quite…

WILLIAM: *Ardea cinerea. Ardea cinerea.*
(*A silence as WILLIAM drifts off into a reverie.*)
I would say that the grey heron is my favourite, then the barn owl, though of course sightings of those are very few and far between, and then maybe the kestrel, the way they hover so skilfully in the wind…

JIM: Yes, I've always liked birds of prey and…

WILLIAM: And I do have something of a passion, I have to confess, for the Manx shearwater. (*After a pause.*) *Puffinus puffinus.*
(*A silence.*)

JIM: So, Bill…how's Jane…?

WILLIAM: Though of course you'll only see that particular bird if you're out in a boat somewhere in the north Atlantic.
(*He laughs slightly. A silence.*)

JIM: Last time I spoke to Cathy she said that…

WILLIAM: You know there's been this huge black crow visiting me lately. Comes most mornings and sits on that tree just there. It's as big as a dog. Never seen anything like it.
(*A silence.*)

JIM: Cathy said that things were…

WILLIAM: My daughter's taking the lead there, Jim. But I think it's all under control.

JIM: Well, I just wanted to say how sorry…

WILLIAM: She doesn't deserve all this, you know. She's a good old girl, is my wife. (*A pause.*) A love.
(*A long silence as WILLIAM peers once again through his binoculars.*)

JIM: And so I hear the firm's still staggering on without you?

WILLIAM: The year I left, Jim, group sales went up nine per cent to 123.7 million, compared with 112.8 million the previous year. It was also the tenth consecutive year of record profits…

JIM: Then you obviously left the place in good…

WILLIAM: Like for like UK sales were up 8.3 per cent. And the average spend per transaction was up to £108 from £99 the year before, with people continuing to upgrade to better quality wines, better quality spirits…

JIM: Well, as I say…

WILLIAM: We opened eight new stores in that financial year and resited two. A pair of chaffinches, I do believe…
(*A silence as he surveys with his binoculars.*)

JIM: Well. You've a lot then to be…

WILLIAM: My cup certainly runs over this morning.

JIM: A lot to be…

WILLIAM: Of course the male has a far more impressive plumage than the female…

(*A silence as WILLIAM continues to look out at the garden, with JIM watching him.*)

JIM: Anyway, Bill, perhaps I'll go inside now and…

WILLIAM: And, most importantly of course, the year I left the dividend was a third higher than in the previous year. Must always keep those shareholders happy, mustn't one?

JIM: You were certainly the man with the Midas touch. You worked hard all your life. Left quite a…

WILLIAM: Worked my way up from unloading vans, stacking shelves, sweeping floors, Jim.

JIM: It's a real success story. You really…

WILLIAM: I did my best.

JIM: You deserve all this opulence, all this…

WILLIAM: I certainly did do my very, very best.

JIM: …all this splendour.

WILLIAM: More to life than money, Jim. Whole lot more to life than a little bit of money.

(*A long silence.*)

JIM: But you must miss the people, surely?

WILLIAM: (*After a pause.*) One or two, I suppose.

(*WILLIAM puts down his binoculars. A long silence.*)

JIM: And you managed to get Richard a job, I heard? At one of the branches?

WILLIAM: (*After a pause.*) Indeed I did.

JIM: Well, that's good. Nice bit of old-fashioned nepotism never harmed any…

WILLIAM: He's assistant manager.

(*A silence.*)

JIM: Well, I'm pleased that he's doing well.

WILLIAM: Doing well, Jim?

JIM: Well, that he's…that he's…happier. Now.

WILLIAM: Are you looking a little older these days?

JIM: I don't know…

WILLIAM: A little greyer, perhaps?

JIM: Well, I suppose it's been a few years since we…

WILLIAM: And what's with the third leg?

JIM: I'm afraid my old rugby injury's finally…

WILLIAM: Game for savages, Jim.

(*A long silence. WILLIAM takes up his binoculars again.*)

JIM: So…do you think Jane might be accepting visitors now or…?

WILLIAM: Cricket is the one true civilised sport. The only sport with real class.

(*A silence.*)

JIM: I really had no idea she was suffering from such a…

WILLIAM: And I had a good team of people under me, Jim, you see. A very good team of people.

JIM: Well, from such a horrible disease.

WILLIAM: I had Mike Tidwell, I had Tom McBurney, I had Steven Dewer. And of course I had the late and great Alexander Stafford.

(*A silence. Inside CATHY has left her mother's room. She sits on the living room sofa and is writing in a note book.*)

JIM: So, if you'll excuse me then, I…

WILLIAM: I also had Pete Slater, I had Simon Redmond, I had that canny Scot Walter McKenzie…

JIM: I'll just…

WILLIAM: I had Colin Mason, I had Eddie Telford, I had the very shapely Linda Harris who was also my personal assistant towards the end of my tenure and, last but by no means least, I had good old Lenny Crapstone.

JIM: (*After a pause.*) I see.

WILLIAM: Good old Lenny Crapstone.

JIM: It's always struck me as remarkable that the man who helped build up one of the country's largest chains of wine warehouses…

WILLIAM: He had a glass eye did Lenny Crapstone.

JIM: …should himself be a lifelong teetotaller…

WILLIAM: I do have my reasons for that.

(*A silence.*)

JIM: So anyway, Bill…if it's all the same to you…I might just pop inside now and say hello to…

WILLIAM: Two years, three months and sixteen days.

JIM: Sorry?

WILLIAM: Two years, three months and sixteen days. Since Richard's been here.

JIM: Right.

WILLIAM: Twenty-one years since all of us were here together. All four of us. Twenty-one Christmases. (*A pause.*) I looked it up.

JIM: Yes, well, I've been really looking forward to seeing how they've both turned out and so…

WILLIAM: I did. I looked it up.

(*A silence.*)

Listen, we must have a game of chess later. Be just like the good old days…

JIM: I don't really think I was much competition for…

WILLIAM: Miss someone to play a good old game of chess with.

(*JIM now escapes inside, WILLIAM looks out at the birds again.*)

I'll follow you in, I'll follow you in…

JIM: This lovely young woman couldn't possibly be Catherine Carmichael, could it?

CATHY: (*Springing to her feet.*) Uncle Jim!

(*She gets up. An awkward moment as he goes to embrace her but she's a little unresponsive.*)

JIM: What a beautiful woman you've become…

CATHY: What rubbish…

JIM: Don't let me interrupt you…

CATHY: Oh, it's nothing really… Just a poem.

JIM: You write poetry?

CATHY: I've been going to these classes but…

JIM: That's wonderful.

CATHY: Been working on this one for a few days. It's about Mum.

JIM: I'd love to hear it.

CATHY: Oh, it's rubbish. I'm a nurse, I'm afraid, not a poet.

(*A silence.*)

JIM: Well…it's lovely to see you again. Really. It's been far too long.

CATHY: I think Dad's outside.

JIM: Just been speaking to him, as a matter of fact.

CATHY: How was he?

JIM: Birdwatching.

CATHY: As ever.

JIM: Always did have a thing for it, didn't he?

CATHY: He's such a worry.

(*A silence.*)

Mum really wanted to see you.

JIM: And I've so wanted to see her. I would have come sooner
but…

CATHY: Can I get you a drink or anything?

JIM: I had a coffee, thanks. Little Chef.

(*A silence.*)

How long have you been back living at home then? When
was she actually diagnosed with this dreadful thing?

CATHY: Three years. It's taken hold quite quickly.

JIM: Cathy, I really wish I'd known sooner…

CATHY: She's been thinking she can beat it. And she didn't
want people to know. But no-one beats it, unfortunately.
It really is an awful way to…an awful way to…

(*A silence.*)

JIM: I'm so sorry. Really. It must be so hard. So hard for you
too. But she's lucky to have a daughter like you. You're
a real credit to her, Cathy. I hope you know that. You do
know that, don't you? You're a real credit to your mother.

(*A silence and then CATHY slowly crumples into gentle tears.
She puts a hand over her face.*

*Outside WILLIAM is still watching the local fauna through his
binoculars.*)

WILLIAM: Starlings times three, wood pigeons times two and
over there the *hirundo rustica*…our good summer visitor the
swallow. Times one.

(*Inside JIM approaches CATHY.*)

JIM: Cathy…

WILLIAM: (*Outside.*) The agility of that flight…

JIM: Listen…

WILLIAM: Go on, my beauty, that's it, that's it…

JIM: I can understand your pain…

WILLIAM: You really are such a beautiful bird.

JIM: But we all have to be brave.

WILLIAM: Catching those flies to take back to the wife and children.

JIM: And try to look upon our pain as a blessing.

WILLIAM: Bringing home the bacon, aren't you, my boy?

JIM: As a blessing from God.

WILLIAM: Bringing home the good old bacon…

(*WILLIAM saunters off, while CATHY recovers slightly.*)

JIM: It's how we grow. Really. It's how we learn. Your pain, your mother's pain, everybody's pain, it's all designed to bring us closer to God. I really believe that this is the case. Forgive me if I speak out of turn but I feel so passionately about this. We are not on our own.

CATHY: I don't really want to talk about God at the moment.

JIM: Some time ago a good friend of mine was diagnosed with cancer. Of the throat. And it really was a terrible time. An absolutely terrible time. For him, of course. And also for his wife, his children, for his parents, his friends. And there was a circle of thirty people and every night we'd pray. On our own or in groups but at exactly the same time each night. We'd pray for him. I know it sounds a little freaky but it isn't really. It's just about energy, transmitting loving energy through your heart and your mind. And we continued this for almost two years, while he was going through all the therapy and all the tests and everything, and then he was pronounced clear. It was like a miracle. How about that then? He was pronounced completely clear of it. And he assured us all that it was the power of our collective prayer that had helped him.

(*No response for a time as JIM beams at her.*)

CATHY: There was no chance then it was the chemotherapy that saved him?

JIM: (*After a pause.*) It is possible, I suppose, but we do prefer to think it was the power of our collective prayer.

CATHY: Well…how is he now?

JIM: He's dead.

CATHY: I'm sorry.

JIM: He died a few months ago.

CATHY: I don't remember you as a religious person.

JIM: I never really was. But in the city…after a few years I think I began to feel a little lost. Lost and alone really. I didn't feel like I really belonged anywhere. I was painfully lonely, I suppose. A country bumpkin in this vast metropolis. And then one day I walked past a young woman handing out leaflets for a church meeting. She was very friendly and seemed so at peace with herself, so totally at ease. She had a big, broad smile, while I was quite depressed at the time and smiling wasn't something I did that much of. And so I went along. I went along for the hell of it and I was simply bowled over by the warmth and the humanity and the generosity of all these people. And I knew from that moment onwards that I'd never ever be alone again. And the rest, as they say, is history. (*After a pause.*) All I wanted to say is that maybe your mother's suffering is a test. Maybe it's simply God's way of…
(*CATHY now turns and walks out of the room.*)
…testing her. Bringing her back to Him, if you like.
(*He looks round to see he is alone.*)

SCENE 4

Twenty years previously. WILLIAM and JANE in the living room, dressed in black. Neither speak for a time.

JANE: Are you alright?

WILLIAM: I'm fine.

JANE: Can I get you anything?

WILLIAM: No.

JANE: Are you sure? I just don't want you to…

WILLIAM: I'm fine.
(*A silence.*)
Why didn't Richard show? You said he knew about it, that Catherine told him. He must have known I'd want him to show.

JANE: It's going to take a little time.

WILLIAM: I wanted him to play. I wanted him to play the piano. I wanted him to play that music. When he was boy, with his teacher, he used to play that lovely music. You remember? He had a real talent. It's what my dad would have liked.

I want him to come home again.

JANE: I know you do so…

WILLIAM: I want to see him again. My…little man.

(*A silence.*)

The money I spent on those piano lessons. All for nothing.

JANE: It wasn't all for nothing.

WILLIAM: Got his talent from my father, didn't he? Missed me out completely. They say he was a good pianist. Before the war. Before the carnage of that desert. Never played again, did he, once he came back. But it was on in the house all the time. Mendelssohn, Bach, Beethoven. On his scratched-up LPs. Odd that is was the German ones he loved the most and it was the Germans that broke his spirit. He'd get drunk, beat me half to death and you know what he'd say as he hit me?

JANE: He'd say you were a waste of…

WILLIAM: 'You're a waste of bloody space, Birdboy! A waste of bloody space!' Then he'd just sit in his room with his battered old gramophone on. Red it was. Red, I remember, against the grubby grey of the walls. And sometimes I looked through the crack in the door and he'd be crying like a baby with all this beautiful music in the air. And then afterwards he'd come looking for me. All red-eyed and pitiful. And he'd just hold me. He'd hold me so tightly I could hardly breathe and he'd say how sorry he was.

JANE: I know…

WILLIAM: 'Sorry, Birdboy. So sorry, my poor little Birdboy.'

JANE: Oh, Bill…

WILLIAM: That's what he'd say.

JANE: You dear, dear man…

WILLIAM: And I could smell it on him, Jane. The Guinness, the red wine, the whiskey. Smell it on him so strong I'd have to hold my breath for minutes at a time.

(*A silence.*)

Maybe I've been too hard on the little man?

JANE: I just think that if you…

WILLIAM: I just wanted him to realise that life is hard. Bloody hard, Jane. It's not a game. The world's not a big playground. The world does not exist solely for his pleasure. Other people do not exist solely for his pleasure. Women do not exist solely for his pleasure. No, it's not a playground. It's a struggle. A long, hard, grim, bloody struggle.

JANE: I'm so worried about you.

WILLIAM: I only wanted him to understand.

JANE: You're working eighty hours a week, you're under a lot of pressure and first Richard and now your father and…

WILLIAM: I only wanted him to understand the way the world works.

JANE: Come on. Sit down.

WILLIAM: For his own good, you understand. So he can survive out there.

JANE: How do you feel about Arthur, Bill? You've not said. You'd not really made your peace with him and so I'm just a little…

WILLIAM: Can't believe he's gone. Can't believe I won't see him again. I won't ever see his face again. His stupid, drunken face.

JANE: I am here for you, you know.

WILLIAM: You're a good woman, Jane. You know that, don't you? I'm a lucky man.

(*A silence.*)

But I feel nothing. Nothing at all.

(*A silence.*)

Nobody there. Was there? Just us. Just you and me and the girl and a few of his drinking pals. And two of them could barely speak. And no-one from his army days even. The man had no friends, had he? No friends at all.

JANE: But he was still your father.

WILLIAM: Now why is that, I ask myself?

JANE: And I know, deep down, he was proud of…

WILLIAM: He never said anything. Never one word of encouragement. Never one word of praise.

JANE: I suspect he was just a little jealous of…

WILLIAM: You hear me laugh, did you? When the vicar came out with that bit about the kindness and generosity hidden underneath all the rage, all the pain? He never was kind to me.

JANE: We do have to remember what he went through.

WILLIAM: Not for a single second was he ever kind to me.

JANE: You need to sit yourself down for a moment. You're getting wound up again.

WILLIAM: He never even met the man, that vicar. Never spent a single bloody minute with him.

JANE: You need to do your breathing…

WILLIAM: The nonsense they come out with…

JANE: You're getting over-excited, darling…

WILLIAM: Dad wouldn't be seen dead in a bloody church anyway.

JANE: Bill, seriously…

WILLIAM: I am not getting 'wound up'!

JANE: Why don't you take off your jacket, have a sit down? I'll do your neck, your shoulders for you?

WILLIAM: Go on then.

JANE: You get so tense, Bill. You need to learn to calm down.

WILLIAM: But I don't need a lecture.

(*WILLIAM takes off his jacket and sits.*)

JANE: And what about your tie then? Why don't you take off your tie?

WILLIAM: I don't want to take off the tie.

JANE: But if you took off your tie…

WILLIAM: But I don't want to take off the tie.

JANE: …you might feel more comfortable.

WILLIAM: It's my cricket club tie is this.

JANE: I know it is.

WILLIAM: But I'll say this for him, that vicar…he does adhere to the correct sport.

JANE: That's good.

(*JANE starts to massage his neck and shoulders.*)

WILLIAM: Had to pull him up sharp on a few points however.
Poor lad was getting a little confused.

JANE: Oh yes?

WILLIAM: In 1975 it was the *West Indies* that won the World
Cup and not Australia. I told him I remember it clearly
and here's how, I said. Because I was at nearly all the
bloody matches! And it was at *Lord's*, not the Oval, where
Lloyd got to a hundred runs off only eighty-two balls. June.
1975. Lords. No doubt about that whatsoever, Jane, but still
he wasn't sure. I'm going to look it up. Double check.
(*JANE now stops massaging him and sighs.*)
He was also labouring under a slight misapprehension
about batting partnerships in the Ashes. He was saying that
Barnes and Bradman in 1946 scored the most runs but in
actual fact it was *Ponsford* and Bradman in 1934. *Ponsford*
and Bradman. Not Barnes and Bradman. Four hundred
and fifty-one, I think they got. Or fifty-two. *Ponsford* and
Bradman and not Barnes and Bradman. I told him to look
it up when he got home and he said he would. I gave him
our number so he could call and offer his apologies to me.
But I suspect he won't. I know it's not so important but
it's always riled me when you're arguing the toss about
something and you know you're right but the other person
just keeps on insisting that they're the one who is right.
(*JANE now picks up his jacket, folds it carefully and exits.*)
I just happen to know these things. First is Ponsford and
Bradman, 1934; then second it's Barnes and Bradman,
1946, then third it's Ponsford and Bradman again, again
in 1934, but this was the fourth test at Headingley and
they scored seventy runs fewer. Then it was Leyland and
Hutton in 1938 at the Oval and fifth it was Graham Gooch
and David Gower just recently. I tell you something, I
half expected Dad to start banging away on the inside of
that coffin. 'It was *Ponsford* and Bradman! You tell him,
Bill! Don't listen to that bloody vicar! It was *Ponsford* and
Bradman, not Barnes and bloody Bradman!'
(*He laughs slightly.*)
Nobody knew their cricket like my old dad.

(*JANE returns.*)

A totally different man. That's what they all said, wasn't it?
Totally different. Before they shipped him off to that desert.
He was a shy, peaceful cricket-loving player of pianos.
You've stopped.

(*She resumes.*)

Yes, I think I'll look it up. Make a photocopy. Not too
hard! You nearly put your thumb through my throat there.
Yes, I'll make a photocopy. Send the proof directly to him.

JANE: Bill, can I ask you something? And I don't want you to
get annoyed.

WILLIAM: Of course I won't get annoyed.

JANE: You say that but…

WILLIAM: I'm telling you I won't get annoyed.

JANE: I was just wondering…

WILLIAM: Why do you always assume I'm going to get
annoyed? That's what I find annoying, Jane. I find it
annoying that you make this assumption that I'm always
going to get annoyed!

JANE: I was thinking that maybe, as regards Rick, if you were
to…apologise to him then…

WILLIAM: Apologise?

JANE: I think if he came home, then he might be persuaded to
finish his A-levels somewhere and then go to college and
then…

WILLIAM: I would like him home, I have to say.

JANE: So, what do you think then? I know he's been difficult,
Bill, but he's at that age and yes, maybe you have been a
little hard on him…but maybe we could put all that behind
us and start again? Start from here? Start from now? But I
really think the first move must come from you.

WILLIAM: We don't even know where he is.

JANE: He's…in London.

WILLIAM: In London? What the hell does he want to be in
London for?

JANE: (*Suddenly upset.*) He's in some horrible squat, Bill. With a
lot of strange people. We don't know what he's going to do
there, what sort of people they are. He needs to be here.

He needs to be here with his mother. He needs to finish his education. Please, Bill…talk to him. I've done all I can to…

WILLIAM: You've spoken to him then?

JANE: (*After a pause.*) He's…been here.

WILLIAM: He's been here? He's been here in this house?

JANE: Yes.

WILLIAM: When was this?

JANE: Monday. He really needed some money.

WILLIAM: (*Standing.*) You what?

JANE: You said you wouldn't get annoyed.

WILLIAM: You gave him money? Do not…for Christ's sake… do not tell me you gave that boy any of my hard-earned money?

JANE: It's our money, Bill. It's our money!

WILLIAM: Did you or did you not give that boy some money?

JANE: It was just a loan, Bill… For goodness sake…

WILLIAM: (*Trying to curb his rage.*) How many times? How many times! That boy is to get nothing. Nothing from me. Nothing at all. I've worked like a slave all my life, since I was sixteen years of age. Work, work, work. You understand. I had nothing from anyone. And I've slogged through it all. I've slogged through the bullshit and the tedium and the backstabbing and the lies and the games they all play and I've done it all for him. For you, for him, for the girl. I've taken nothing for myself, nothing at all, and that little bastard, that arrogant lazy little bastard…

JANE: Bill, please…

WILLIAM: Don't you touch me! Don't touch me…

JANE: Please, you need to calm down…

WILLIAM: It's the best school in the country. It's the best in the country by a bloody mile and I've paid through the nose for it. And I had nothing and what does he think? What does he care? He throws it all back in my face with that arrogant shrug, with that arrogant smirk. Well, we'll see. We'll see what happens to him! Because you mark my words, one day, one fine day, that little bugger will come crawling back here. And he'll be all head bowed and scraping and he'll be begging for forgiveness but he'll get nothing. He'll get nothing from me because I've done all the giving I've got in me! Because it's the gutter, it's the gutter is where he's headed. Some dead-end low-paid grind of a job. And I tell you something else: he'll deserve it. He bloody well deserves everything he gets…

JANE: Please…

(*Meanwhile JIM comes onto the terrace with a bouquet of flowers.*)

WILLIAM: And how much did you give him? How much of my money did you actually give him?

JANE: It was nothing…

(*JIM stops in his tracks when he hears the raised voices coming from the house.*)

WILLIAM: Tell me, you'd better tell me now! How much of my money did you give to him…

JANE: I'm sorry…

WILLIAM: Answer me!

JANE: It was nothing, Bill, I just thought…

WILLIAM: (*Grabbing her.*) Answer me now, or I swear to God, I'll…

JANE: You're hurting me…

WILLIAM: How much of my money did you give him…

JANE: I'm sorry, I'm sorry, I'm sorry…

WILLIAM: (*Exploding.*) ANSWER THE QUESTION NOW!
(*JIM is in an agony of indecision. First approaching the house and then walking away.*)

JANE: It was just five hundred pounds.

WILLIAM: Five hundred pounds!? You gave him five hundred pounds!?

JANE: You're hurting me, Bill, you're really hurting me…
(*He releases her and then rages around the room.*)

WILLIAM: Jesus Christ! You gave him five hundred pounds? You gave him five hundred pounds of my money! I don't believe it! Behind my back! Behind my back! I told you I didn't want him setting foot in this house and then you go and invite him in and you give him my money!

JANE: He just turned up, Bill! What could I…

WILLIAM: Shut up! Yes? You understand! Shut your mouth! Shut your bloody mouth!

JANE: I'm his mother, Bill. What kind of mother would just...

WILLIAM: You gave him money! You gave him my money! My money! Yes? You gave him my money! Jesus Christ! I tell you something, I've had it now! I've had it with the whole bloody lot of you!

(*He storms out of the room. A silence descends.*
Alone inside, JANE in a state of shock.
Outside, JIM is still wavering. Then JANE sees him. She steps outside onto the terrace. A long silence.)

JIM: Is everything alright? I heard shouting. Not sure...not sure what to do. Exactly. Coming over to offer my condolences to Bill actually. But I think I'd better just go. Sorry to intrude. I can see you're upset. I don't like to see you upset.

(*A silence.*)

I also came over to apologise to you for what happened. Is this the right time?

(*She does not respond.*)

I've been keeping away from you, Jane, because I feel so mortally ashamed of my conduct. I don't know what came over me but I desperately hope it won't jeopardise our friendship.

(*She does not respond.*)

The friendship I have with you is the most important thing in my life. Truthfully. And it was madness on my part to do anything to endanger it. I really don't know what came over me. Really. Please say you'll forgive me.

(*A silence.*)

Did he hurt you? Does he ever hurt you? I couldn't bear it if he hurts you. I really couldn't. It's not my business but, well it is my business I suppose because I really do... I really do... But does he ever...? Has he ever...? Look, I'd better just go. Here. Sorry.

(*He gives her the flowers and then turns and walks out. Alone, JANE looks off after JIM. She then turns. She goes back inside where she is met by a contrite-looking WILLIAM.*)

A long, long silence.)

WILLIAM: I'm sorry. I don't seem to be able to control my
temper, do I? And God knows, I try. But sometimes the
red mist descends and I'm lost. So I'm sorry, Jane. It won't
happen again. Nice flowers. Really…nice. Are they for…?
(*JANE now starts walking away.*)
Oh, please don't walk away. I don't want to be on my own.
I'm just upset about Dad and there's a film on tonight.
A James Bond. Why don't we watch that? Or we could go
out? We've not been out to eat together for months. What
you say?
(*She walks off.*)
I really am sorry! It won't happen again. I swear to you…
I've my hand on my heart, look…I swear to you that it
won't ever, ever happen again.
(*He is alone. He looks sadly about the room. He then is about
to leave when he walks over to the piano in the corner. He sits
at the seat, opens up the piano and starts to hit the keys, slowly,
listlessly, like a child. He has no musical ability. He continues
until:*)
Can't really do anything, can you, old son? Can't really do
anything at all in this stupid bloody life.

SCENE 5

*The present. Birdsong. Alone, JANE sits in a wheelchair on the terrace,
looking out. We see she has occasional spasming in one arm and in one
leg. After a time CATHY comes out to her.*

CATHY: He's on his way down.
JANE: It's amazing how much goes on out here, when you
can't move. You notice everything. Just sitting here
like this. The light, it changes. Almost every moment.
Something different. All these colours, the different greens,
the browns. How sad that I've not really noticed any of this
before.
CATHY: Was it nice to see Uncle Jim again?
JANE: Watching all the light move.
CATHY: Dad's showing him the sunflowers.
JANE: And the wind through the leaves.

CATHY: Seems to have found God.

JANE: Such a shame. This garden. So huge. Seems so huge now we don't have you two running about, playing football, playing tennis, splashing in the pool, with all your friends from school.

CATHY: I don't really remember…

JANE: Especially during the summer. Laughing and shouting. Rick's terrible band practising in the attic. Seems so vast now, the garden. Doesn't it? So empty. So overgrown.

CATHY: He really needs to get someone in to…

JANE: Just does his broad beans and his sunflowers. Every year. Broad beans and sunflowers. Exactly like his father. (*A pause.*) Yes. This is the first time I've really just sat still and looked.

CATHY: How are you feeling?

JANE: And actually listened.

CATHY: Is this still what you want? Tonight?

JANE: What *have* I been doing with all my time?

CATHY: Is it?

JANE: He's had his problems, your father, but you do have to admit that he's done well for himself. Started out with nothing at all…

CATHY: I'm just not sure if you should…

JANE: I know what's coming. And you know. It's absolutely awful and cruel and rotten. But I want no-one to know. Like we said. We have tonight. We have a nice night tonight, you help me to bed and then we…and then I…

(*RICHARD, hungover, now comes out onto terrace.*)

RICHARD: And then you what?

JANE: Come over here then, my darling, and let me have a good look at you.

(*RICHARD goes over to his mother. He kneels down by the wheelchair.*)

My little treasure…

RICHARD: How you doing?

JANE: (*To CATHY.*) Are you not making a coffee for your brother then?

CATHY: I don't think I am, no.

RICHARD: Coffee would be great actually.

CATHY: Well, you know where the kitchen is.

JANE: Oh, please don't be so mean.

CATHY: Can't he make one himself?

JANE: He had a long drive last night.

CATHY: I'm sorry but I'm not just going to be his personal…

JANE: Then I'll have one as well, please…

(CATHY angrily leaves the terrace.)

So where is that adorable son of yours then? I assumed he'd be up rampaging around by now? Of course poor little Thongbai is as quiet as a mouse but that boy, so full of life…

RICHARD: Mum…

JANE: Your father doesn't know, does he? That you've been coming here? Because it would so break his heart.

RICHARD: No.

JANE: And he'd get so cross with me, you see…

RICHARD: I don't want him being cross with you…

JANE: He loves you so much. You just have to understand how hard things were for him when…

RICHARD: Don't want to talk about it.

JANE: And have you seen him yet?

RICHARD: Last night.

JANE: And how was it?

RICHARD: Don't want to talk about it.

JANE: I'm so pleased you're happier now. You've found a direction at last, you've got this good job and your son and your wife. Because you've always been so lost, haven't you? Never knowing what you're doing really and we've been so worried. And I can't tell you what it means to us to know that you're finally happy. Really, Rick, I can go peacefully now.

RICHARD: But I don't want you to go.

JANE: Come here then…

(RICHARD puts his head on her lap and she strokes his hair.)

My beautiful boy, weren't you?

RICHARD: About Jack…

JANE: How I miss the baby that you were. Sitting out here, picking up the dirt, your little wrists, your fat little knees. Those delightful sounds you used to make. And kissing the back of your neck. I'd sit out here and kiss the back of your neck for hours on end. You were my best friend really. I so so miss the baby that you were.

(*CATHY returns to the terrace with the coffee and stands behind them.*)

Your sister was a lot more spiky. Such a troubled child. Always wriggling off you when you went to pick her up. Never wanted to join in much. I'm so grateful to her. She says she won't go back to her old job when I'm gone and so what is she going to do? She still talks about volunteering in Kenya or somewhere but I can't see it, can you? At the moment she seems happy looking after me and writing these peculiar poems. But, between you and me, I'm not sure if it'll lead to anything.

RICHARD: Mum, I hate to ask you again but you couldn't see your way clear to lending me a...

JANE: Oh, Richard...I've given you all that I have. I have no access to any money now. None at all. He controls all...

RICHARD: Of course not. Sorry.

(*Enter WILLIAM and JIM from the garden.*)

WILLIAM: ...and so at this time of year your visible constellations are as follows: Ursa Minor, Polaris, Ursa Major. Then you've got Vega-alpha, Arcturus, Leo and Hercules. Then of course you've got Spica, Virgo and Corvus. You've got Antares and Scorpius. And last but by no means least, Jim, you've got good old Sagittarius.

JIM: I see.

WILLIAM: And so that's the question, isn't it: in a world like ours that's in utter chaos, politically and environmentally, how can the human race possibly sustain another hundred years?

JIM: But if you're such an advocate of the capitalist system...

WILLIAM: Simple. We're going to have to jump ship. Settle ourselves on another planet altogether.

JIM: Surely capitalism is responsible for much of this...

WILLIAM: Because people's selfishness, people's intrinsic greed…

JIM: But there's a contradiction at the heart of your argument, Bill…

WILLIAM: If you'd just let me make my point…

JIM: (*Laughing, to others.*) Just debating the end of the world.

WILLIAM: Every night I look out at the wonderful vastness of the universe and I know, I simply know, Jim, that somewhere out there, somewhere out there, there simply has to be…

JANE: Isn't this lovely then? I'm surrounded by all the people I love in this world. All the people I think I've ever loved. And, what is more, what is even nicer, is that I'm surrounded by all the people who I think truly love me. (*Nobody speaks.*)

End of Act One.

Act Two

SCENE 1

The present. Evening. JANE, WILLIAM and JIM are seated at the table on the terrace. RICHARD is inside on his mobile, having a drink. As the act starts CATHY is helping her mother finish her meal. All watch her as they struggle. When CATHY finishes this she begins clearing plates from the terrace and taking them through the living room and off. She comes back and forward throughout.

WILLIAM: My point was, Jim, that the greatest prosperity and standard of living in any society can only be attained through capitalism…

RICHARD: (*Inside, on his phone.*) If you're going to shout at me… If you're going to shout at me then you'll have to speak English…

CATHY: (*Entering the room with plates etc.*) You alright in here?

WILLIAM: (*Outside.*) …and that's because under capitalism the incentives to produce and create and innovate are unhindered by government regulation or mandate.

CATHY: (*Muttering as she exits.*) You take it easy then, Richard. You just leave everything to me…

RICHARD: (*On phone again.*) Alright so…if you're talking in Thai then please do it slowly.

JIM: (*Outside.*) Yes, but surely…

WILLIAM: And when government does prohibit or limit business activity, or when it confiscates a significant portion of the product of your labour through taxes, there is little or no incentive to produce or to create or to innovate.

RICHARD: (*Inside, on phone.*) But I love you, not her!

WILLIAM: No doubt folk like my son wouldn't agree. He thinks the purpose of life is to bum around on a beach all day, indulging yourself, but look where that's got him.

JIM: Well, I'm not a businessman in the strict sense of the word but I've always had to try and sell my…

WILLIAM: It's about freedom. A capitalist system recognises that men are free, thinking beings. Agreed?

RICHARD: (*Inside, on phone.*) Because I can't sleep on his sofa any more!

JIM: The problem with…

WILLIAM: A man must think for himself, choose his own path in life, and act accordingly to pursue the goals he's chosen. Use his reason to discover the truth and be responsible…

JIM: But if, as you said before, we've destroyed the…

WILLIAM: Like I've been. Like you've been, Jim.

RICHARD: (*Inside, on phone.*) Then you have to forgive me and let me come home!

WILLIAM: (*Outside.*) Capitalism allows a man to think and act freely. It allows him to work in whichever profession he wants, buy and sell whatever he wants, say what he wants, worship the god he wants, and pursue his own definition of happiness.

JANE: (*To CATHY who is now back outside.*) The thing to remember about men is that, when they get to a certain age, they simply can't ever stop talking.

JIM: Happiness, you say?

WILLIAM: Happiness, yes. That's what it all boils down to.

RICHARD: (*Inside, on phone.*) But I didn't, I swear!

CATHY: Can I get anyone anything else?

WILLIAM: That was smashing.

JIM: Wonderful, thank you.

WILLIAM: No, just the bill, please… (*A pause. A slight laugh.*) Coffee. Sorry, love. Just the coffees.
(*A silence as CATHY collects more crockery etc and clears away.*)

JIM: (*To JANE.*) You alright there?

JANE: It's such a lovely evening, isn't it?

JIM: It is.

JANE: Such a deep, dark sky.

JIM: Another starry one for you, Bill?

WILLIAM: It is amazing to know that when a lot of this starlight left its various sources, there were probably dinosaurs gallumphing about down there, where my broad beans and my sunflowers are.

(They all gaze up at the sky. Nobody speaks. It is clear that JANE and JIM long to talk but feel unable to in WILLIAM's presence. Meanwhile, CATHY comes inside, carrying her tray of dirty plates. Her path is blocked by her brother.)

RICHARD: I'm in big trouble.

CATHY: Are you going to come back outside?

RICHARD: Oh Jesus…

CATHY: You know he just asked me for the bill!

RICHARD: I need to talk to someone.

CATHY: You're drunk.

RICHARD: I had sex with a girl. From work. Just once. And then she got all obsessed with me and told Thongbai.

CATHY: And now she's thrown you out?

RICHARD: And now she's gone to the police. She's saying I forced myself… I swear I didn't. Never in my life have I even come close to…

CATHY: I don't believe this…

RICHARD: And it was me that tried to resist her.

CATHY: I can't listen to this.

RICHARD: But she had her hands all over me…

CATHY: I said I can't listen to this…

RICHARD: How can she do that to me?

CATHY: Were you drunk?

RICHARD: Why would she say that? Why would she lie?

CATHY: Excuse me.

RICHARD: She was sexy. She was fun. And I thought it was just…you know. I know it was wrong. But she knew I was married.

CATHY: I'm making the coffee.

RICHARD: What do I do?

CATHY: *(Exiting.)* I said I'm making the coffee…

RICHARD: *(Following her off.)* I need someone to help me, Cath. I need someone to tell me what to do.

(An awkward silence outside on the terrace.)

JIM: *(To JANE.)* It's lovely to see you again.

JANE: And it's lovely to see you.

(The silence continues.)

JIM: It's a beautiful night.

JANE: It really is.

(*The silence continues.*
Then CATHY *comes back into the room, followed by her*
brother.)

CATHY: Richard, you asked me for money last night!

RICHARD: Did I?

CATHY: And you're going to have to tell her. You'll have to tell her they're not coming.

RICHARD: Will you tell her…

CATHY: I can't believe this.

RICHARD: I don't know what to do. I just don't know what to do in this life.

CATHY: Be a man, Richard. Be a grown-up man.

RICHARD: I'm trying.

CATHY: Just come outside…

RICHARD: It's Dad. I just can't stand him. I can't stand to be in his company.

CATHY: Then can't you at least do what I do and smile for the cameras?

RICHARD: I feel out of control.

CATHY: I'm sorry about that.

RICHARD: I need someone to talk to. I need my family…

CATHY: Listen. Mum is dying. You understand? And this evening is supposed to be for her. For her to be happy in. And you are drunk. She's dying and you're drunk. And I cannot, I simply cannot deal with another one of your crises. Not tonight…

(*She goes back out onto the terrace and starts to clear up more of*
the dishes, bowls, etc. Alone in the room, RICHARD *sits on the*
sofa, nursing his drink.)

JIM: (*Outside.*) Here she comes again. Here comes the little miracle-worker!

CATHY: If you could just pass me that.

JIM: Nurse by day, chef by night, is it?

JANE: A cleaner, a waitress, a chauffeur…

WILLIAM: Yes, she's a good old girl. Aren't you? A good old girl.

CATHY: If you say so.

WILLIAM: A love.

JANE: You know she writes poems too?

CATHY: Mum, please…

JANE: And they're terribly good.

JIM: She was working on one earlier.

JANE: She's been going to these classes.

JIM: I'd love to hear one if you…

JANE: I've been trying but I'm not very good.

JIM: Well, I think your mother would love to…

WILLIAM: Can't see the point in poems myself. I see some of them printed in the newspapers and most of them don't make any sense at all. Half of them don't even rhyme.

JIM: I don't think it's always necessary for…

WILLIAM: A poem has to rhyme or it's not a poem, is it?

CATHY goes back inside with the remainder of crockery etc.

Now your limerick on the other hand…

An awkward silence outside, while CATHY passes her brother on the sofa.

RICHARD: Cath?

CATHY: (*Exiting.*) I'm making the coffee.

(*The silence continues to build outside as RICHARD, inside, sits with his head in his hands. Then:*)

WILLIAM: A lonely sheep herder from Texas,

Doesn't know what conventional sex is,

He will grab for release

Anything that has fleece,

Caring not what the sex he selects is.

(*WILLIAM laughs. No-one else does. The laugh peters out. Then a long, awkward silence.*

CATHY now returns through the living room. She stops by her brother.)

CATHY: I'm begging you, come outside.

RICHARD: How long has she got?

CATHY: Stay with it tonight, please. Pretend to be happy tonight. Just for God's sake don't tell her about your new little problem…

RICHARD: How long?

CATHY: (*After a pause.*) Not very long.

RICHARD: What happens then? How does it happen?

CATHY: I've told you. Her muscles are weakening, she's finding it more and more difficult to breathe. She'll die from respiratory failure, her chest muscles will stop working and she'll suffocate, choke. It's not nice…

RICHARD: I don't want her to die.

CATHY: Just be happy tonight then. Okay? Do it for her. Do it for me. Be happy and charming and light. Just for one night. Can you do that?

RICHARD: I don't know.

CATHY: Will you try to do that for her? She's your mother and she loves you. You're the one she loves more than anyone else. You know that. So just…pretend. Okay?

RICHARD: Okay.

CATHY: Take this outside and drink lots of it yourself. (*She hands him the tray with the coffee and cups etc.*) Try and sober up.

RICHARD: Yes. Sorry. I will. Sorry.

(*CATHY goes back off to the kitchen.*
RICHARD, alone in the room, braces himself.)
(*To himself.*) Be happy then. Be happy. Be charming. Be light.
(*RICHARD now comes outside, holding the tray.*)

JIM: Ah, the return of the prodigal son!

RICHARD: Mum, Dad, Uncle Jim… I just wanted to say… I just wanted to say how happy I am that we're all here tonight and…
(*He loses his footing as he approaches them and falls onto the table, knocking it over and crashing onto the ground.*
CATHY now returns from the house with a small sugar bowl and steps out onto the terrace.)

CATHY: I wasn't sure if anyone takes…if anyone takes…
(*She breaks off as she is confronted by the sight of her brother sprawling about on the ground.*
Nobody speaks.)

SCENE 2

The past. The living room. JANE and JIM, both standing. A long silence.

JANE: I don't know what to say.

JIM: I thought maybe I'd just go and…disappear. But then I thought no, it would only be right and proper to say goodbye.

JANE: Where are you going?

JIM: London. It'll be a struggle, I suppose… It'll be a real struggle but I need a challenge. I need to get away from here anyway. You understand.

JANE: I've been wanting to get away all my life.

JIM: It's beautiful and quiet and there's a lot about it I like but I'm lonely, I suppose. I'm lonely and uninspired and slowly getting older and maybe I can be happier in the city. Join this big party that always seems to be going on.

JANE: Always wanted to have a bash at London.

JIM: I'm such a boring person, Jane. I'm so bourgeois and boring and I just need to throw myself into the unknown, I think.

JANE: What about me?

JIM: What about you?

JANE: What will I do without you?

JIM: You'll be fine.

JANE: You're my best friend.

JIM: I'm sure you'll be…

JANE: I suddenly feel so…bereft. So alone in the world.

JIM: I'm sorry.

JANE: Is this because of what happened before?

JIM: (*After a pause.*) Partly.

JANE: That was nothing. We can forget all about it surely?

JIM: I don't think I can.

JANE: But I don't want you to just go. I need you. I need you as a friend.

JIM: I don't think I can be your friend.

JANE: Please don't say that.

JIM: And I can't see you any more. Really. I shan't be able to…shan't be able to see you. I'd better just go. I'm becoming a little bit…a little bit…

JANE: You don't want to see me again?

JIM: No. And I'm going to go now…

JANE: But, Jim, I don't want you to go.

JIM: The fact is I'm in love with you. And I've been fighting it for nearly twenty years. It's the reason my marriage failed, it's the reason my life is so empty. I love you and… I know it's hopeless because I can't offer you anything. I'm this middle-class fool, this failure really, and how do I compete with Bill? He's a real man, isn't he? He's started with nothing, fought his way up against all that brutal parenting and he's built all this from nothing and you, you are his reward. You and all this. I was just born into it. I've earned no money of my own, I just sit about in my inherited property pretending to be an artist. I've no great mark to make on this world sadly, nothing interesting to say. But I do love you. That I know. I know that you and I…if things had been different… I know that you're unhappy and God knows I am and sometimes I have this mad vision of how the future could be. You and I. But that's not to be…and I can't bear to be just your friend. Not any more. It's been two decades of torture for me and I kick myself that I didn't say any of this a long time ago when there might have been a chance but…

(*A silence.*)

So now I have to go.

(*A silence.*)

I'll always love you. (*A pause.*) Please be happy.

(*Sadly he turns to go. He walks away. Then:*)

JANE: Take me with you.

(*JIM stops and turns.*)

JIM: I beg your pardon?

JANE: I said, take me with you.

(*She approaches him.*)

JIM: But what about your son, your daughter…?

JANE: Please. Just…take me with you.

(*A long silence.*
She walks to him and comes very close to him.
Nervously and slowly he opens his arms.
She walks into them.
He holds her.)

JIM: I suddenly feel happier than I've ever felt before in my entire…in my entire…in my entire…
(*He continues to hold her.*)

SCENE 3

The present. WILLIAM and RICHARD are outside. RICHARD very drunk. Neither speak for some time.

RICHARD: I'll get you another one.

WILLIAM: Think I can just about stretch to a new cafetière and a few coffee cups.
(*The silence builds.*)
You feeling better now?

RICHARD: I'm alright.
(*The silence builds.*)

WILLIAM: You remember your Uncle Jim of course?

RICHARD: I'm not drunk.

WILLIAM: (*After a pause.*) Of course not.
(*The silence builds.*)
He's a good man. Very good to your mother.
(*The silence builds.*)
Little bird tells me your branch is doing quite well?

RICHARD: Is it?

WILLIAM: What, you mean you don't know?

RICHARD: No.

WILLIAM: You mean you don't know your own branch sales?

RICHARD: Haven't got a clue.

WILLIAM: But you're assistant manager, aren't you?

RICHARD: What it says on my little red badge.

WILLIAM: You must know surely? It's the job of the…
(*WILLIAM checks himself. The silence builds. It's a long one.*)
Anyway, how's the music going?

RICHARD: It isn't.

WILLIAM: Well, you should keep it up. You had a real talent at your music.

RICHARD: Going nowhere.

WILLIAM: Well, at least as a hobby then or…

RICHARD: Not good enough.

WILLIAM: All the drivel that passes as music these days, I would have thought your lot could easily have… (*He breaks off.*) Anyway. We thought you were good. Or at least your mother did.

(*The silence builds.*)

She's always going on about it. Missing the rumpus from the attic. You and your mates with your funny hair-dos and your daft make-up.

(*The silence builds.*)

How *are* your mates? Luke, was it, that your sister liked and Andy and that coloured lad with all that curly hair and…?

(*A pause.*) You seen any of them recently? You were a real close-knit gang, weren't you? I always envied you your mates.

RICHARD: Haven't seen any of them for…

WILLIAM: Never too good at making friends myself. When I was that age.

RICHARD: You preferred your birds.

WILLIAM: I preferred my birds.

(*The silence builds.*)

I'd just like to say, though, that your mother and I…we're really pleased you finally came home. You came home from your travels and you decided to make a fist of it in this country. Because the music and the barwork was all well and good but it was only a stop-gap, wasn't it? It was never going to be…you know…your actual life, was it?

RICHARD: It *was* my life.

WILLIAM: But what I mean is…this is where you belong. This country. England. It's your home. It's your country and it's given you a lot. Your place is here. With your family, your friends.

RICHARD: Don't have any friends here.

WILLIAM: But you have us, don't you?

RICHARD: Because they've all…succeeded.

(*The silence builds.*)

WILLIAM: It's a good company, you know. You start at the bottom but you can work your way up. Good pension, decent benefits. It's not the rock'n'roll lifestyle maybe but it is safe. And that's not to be sniffed at. Not at your age. Not with a wife and a kiddie and everything. I know the pay isn't great at the moment but it will be. You keep your head down and work hard, make the right noises at the right times, show that you're keen and there'll be openings. Of course you are a bit behind other men of your age, salary-wise but, as I say, if you work hard, if you keep your nose to the grindstone… Well, look at me. Look at where I started. They used to look down at me, to begin with. They did. You know what they used to call me?

RICHARD: Not Warehouse Willy, was it?

WILLIAM: Warehouse Willy. But I knew where I was going. I was going right to the top. I was going to show everyone what I could do. I was going to show the whole world that William Carmichael wasn't just a waste of space. And see where I ended up.

(*The silence builds.*)

And, of course, there's no harm in me putting in the odd word for you every so often, is there?

(*He puts his hand on RICHARD's shoulder, who instinctively pulls away.*
The silence builds.)

How's that…that lovely Thai bride of yours then…?

RICHARD: (*After a pause.*) She's fine.

WILLIAM: And that grandson of mine is…?

RICHARD: He's fine.

(*The silence builds.*)

WILLIAM: I did see something in the shop. For the lad. But in the end, I just wasn't sure if…

RICHARD: You said.

WILLIAM: Wasn't sure whether or not it would be quite appropriate so…

(*The silence builds.*)

Is everything alright? At home…?

RICHARD: Everything's fine.

(*The silence builds.*)

WILLIAM: I do know how it can be, you know. Bringing up a family. Especially with us men. We can feel…trapped. As the years pass by… I've been there myself so… And we have to be strong. You know, to overcome ourselves. Our…animal urges, so to speak. So, if you ever need to talk or…

RICHARD: I don't need to talk.

WILLIAM: You don't need to talk?

(*The silence builds.*)

Started shelling my broad beans this week.

(*The silence builds.*)

You remember helping me with that? When you were a lad?

RICHARD: No.

WILLIAM: You don't remember?

RICHARD: No.

WILLIAM: Oh, come on. We always used to love to…

(*The silence builds.*)

RICHARD: Where's Mum?

WILLIAM: She's having a chat with Jim.

RICHARD: I'll go and see if she…

WILLIAM: Better leave them, son.

RICHARD: Why's that?

WILLIAM: It's just that…they haven't seen each other for quite a few years and so…it might be kind to let them…

RICHARD: Kind?

WILLIAM: Kind. Yes.

RICHARD: And you know about that, do you?

(*The silence builds.*)

WILLIAM: All I'm saying is…

RICHARD: Then I'll go and help my sister with the…

WILLIAM: I'm sure she can manage.

(*The silence builds.*)

Two years, three months and sixteen days.

RICHARD: Sorry?

WILLIAM: Since you were last here. Two years, three months and sixteen days. (*A pause.*) I looked it up.
(*The silence builds.*)

RICHARD: I don't want her to die.

WILLIAM: Sorry?
(*The silence builds.*)
And you alright for money?

RICHARD: (*After a pause.*) I'm fine.

WILLIAM: Because… I don't want that grandson of mine to go without.

RICHARD: You've helped us enough.

WILLIAM: Well, the house is a sound investment but…

RICHARD: I'm alright.

WILLIAM: Good lad, good lad… You're doing just fine then.
(*The silence builds.*)
You know what your grandfather always used to say to me? 'Bricks and mortar, bricks and mortar. You've nothing in this life if you've no bricks and mortar.' (*He laughs slightly.*) You know you got your talent from him? Your talent with the piano.

RICHARD: I have no talent.

WILLIAM: Bricks and mortar, bricks and mortar…
(*The silence builds.*)
Should have listened more to his advice. Should have put my money in good old property. Not in these daft stocks and shares. (*Laughing.*) Had tens of thousands wiped off the other month.
(*The silence builds.*)
Maybe…later…we could have that game of chess?

RICHARD: I'll play you for money! Five hundred quid.

WILLIAM: On second thoughts I don't think you're in a fit state to…

RICHARD: One game. I'm white. Five hundred quid.
(*The silence builds.*)

WILLIAM: I'll think about it…
(*The silence builds.*)

Did I tell you? There's been this huge black crow visiting me lately. Massive. As big as a dog. Never seen anything like it.

(*RICHARD comes inside and finds his drink. Pacing in the room, he dials a number on his mobile.*)

(*Not noticing his son's absence.*) See my box up there? Family of blue tits set up shop in it. Delighted. I've got blue tits in that one, sparrows in that one there and a pair of robins in the old one on the willow tree. You and I put that one up together. Summer of '76. June the Fifth. (*After a pause.*) I looked it up.

(*JIM comes onto the terrace, pushing JANE in her wheelchair.*)

WILLIAM: Everything alright?

JANE: I'm bearing up.

WILLIAM: Good girl.

(*Inside, with mounting frustration, RICHARD dials again. On the terrace nobody speaks until:*)

JANE: It's such a lovely evening, isn't it? Everything's just so…just so perfect tonight.

(*Inside, CATHY comes through the living room.*)

CATHY: (*To RICHARD.*) You going to be sociable then?

(*RICHARD holds up a dismissive hand. She leaves him and comes out onto the terrace.*)

JANE: Where's your brother?

CATHY: He's just coming.

WILLIAM: You know, love, he was just telling me how much happier he is these days.

JANE: Really?

CATHY: It's true, Mum.

JANE: Jack and Thongbai are ill, you say?

CATHY: It seems so.

(*The silence builds.*)

Listen, I'm not really sure about this.

JIM: We'd love to hear it, really.

CATHY: I've never read one out before.

JIM: I'm sure your mother would love it too.

CATHY: This is probably my best one then. It's called 'Mother Earth' and…well, I hope you like it.

(*She takes out a small pad from her pocket. She clears her throat. A silence then:*)

You gave unto me the sweet gift of my birth,

Oh Mother, dear Mother, oh Mother of this earth,

You gave me the sunlight, you gave me the seas,

You gave me the air and the grass and the trees…

RICHARD: (*Inside, on the phone, shouting.*) But you have to hear me out!

(*A silence. They all look towards the house. Then:*)

CATHY: You gave me the seasons, the cold and the heat,

The courage to fight and to brook no defeat,

My blood is your blood and my breath is your breath…

RICHARD: (*Inside, on the phone.*) Because I fucking love you!!

(*A long silence. They all look towards the house. Then:*)

WILLIAM: Go on, love… Don't worry about your brother…

CATHY: My blood is your blood and my breath is your breath…

From the day I was born to the day of my death,

You're deep in my heart and you're deep in my soul…

RICHARD: (*Inside, on the phone, a cry of despair.*) I want to come home! I just want to come home and see my fucking son!

(*A silence. They all look towards the house. Then:*)

CATHY: You're deep in my heart and you're deep in my soul…

Without you I'm empty but with you I'm whole.

You gave unto me the sweet gift of my birth,

Oh Mother, dear Mother, oh Mother of this earth.

(*Nobody speaks. CATHY has become very moved. She looks up for a response. They all look at their feet.*

After a time, RICHARD, angry and upset, comes out onto the terrace.)

JIM: Cathy, that was really very…

RICHARD: (*Swaying dangerously.*) She can't take him back there, Mum. Says she's taking him to Bangkok. He's mine. He's my son and he's all I've got and I want to see my little man…my little man, my little man.

(*Silence as they all stare at him as he sways.*)

SCENE 4

The past. JANE stands in the living room, with her coat on, two large suitcases standing by. She is re-reading a letter. She then puts it in an envelope, seals it and places it on the sofa. She looks around the room sadly. She checks her watch and then makes her way through onto the terrace with the cases. As she does so she is startled to hear the familiar sound of a car stopping to a halt on the gravel. Her expression of horror as WILLIAM now comes on with a large bouquet of flowers, identical to the one JIM brought her earlier.

WILLIAM: (*Entering.*) Just caught you! They went and cancelled the bloody thing so I thought I'd come home and surprise you. (*He hands her the flowers.*) I'm pleased because the last thing I feel like doing is spending a week in Germany, with a lot of drunken businessmen. So, I thought I'd take you out. We'd go up to London. See a musical maybe, a Lloyd Webber maybe and then have something to eat, stay in a nice hotel. Spend some of this hard-earned money of mine! Yes, you know where you are with a Lloyd Webber. I know I've been a misery of late and so I'm going to make it up to you. We'll have some good old-fashioned fun.
(*A long silence as he takes in what's happening.*)
Where are you off to? You've bags packed? So you were taking a secret trip yourself? (*A pause. A mood change.*) Look, I don't mind. You need the odd break of course you do but…for God's sake, you don't have to arrange these things behind my back. All you have to do is ask. I won't be angry. Just tell me so's I know. So's I know when it shows up on the statement.

JANE: Bill…

WILLIAM: So where were you off to?

JANE: I'm leaving you.
(*He does not respond.*)
I'm leaving you and I'm not coming back.
(*He does not respond.*)
I wanted to get away while you were abroad and while Cathy was with her friend. I've letters for you both inside. I don't love you, Bill. Not any more. I'm unhappy and I have been for a long time. I just can't do this. I need to find

my own life. Whatever that is. Find my own way. While
there's still time.
(*He does not respond.*)
I'm lonely, Bill. I've been so lonely and scared for so long
and I know I'm not making the most of my life. It's all
going past so quickly and I feel cut off from things. I don't
know what I'm going to do but I just know I have to go.
(*He does not respond.*)
I don't want any of your money. I don't want anything
from you. Just to be happy. And just for you to be happy.
I so want you to be happy because…because you so, so
deserve to be.
(*She picks up her cases and slowly walks past him.*
He puts out a hand and holds her by the arm.)

WILLIAM: Don't…

JANE: Bill, please…

WILLIAM: Don't go…

JANE: I'm going.

WILLIAM: Is there another man?

JANE: (*After a pause.*) I just need to be alone.

WILLIAM: You're leaving me for no-one?

JANE: I'm leaving you for no-one.

WILLIAM: Why would you just leave me for no-one?

JANE: I need to be…

WILLIAM: You don't want to be on your own, do you?

JANE: Please…let go of my arm.

WILLIAM: Not at your age? Why be on your own at your age?

JANE: Please…

WILLIAM: I don't want you to go.

JANE: It's in the letter.

WILLIAM: Twenty years.

JANE: I'm sorry.

WILLIAM: Twenty bloody years, love.

JANE: We've not been happy.

WILLIAM: Over just like that?

JANE: We've neither of us been happy.

WILLIAM: I don't want you to go…

JANE: Be honest.

WILLIAM: I really don't want you to go.

JANE: Be honest with yourself.

WILLIAM: I can't have this. I really can't be having this, love.

(*A long silence. He stares at her, she avoids his eyes.*)

JANE: I'll be in touch. In a few weeks. Look after yourself.

(*She picks up her bags and begins to leave. Then:*)

WILLIAM: Jane?

(*She slowly turns back to him.*)

(*Slowly, calmly.*) Please don't go. I need you. You're the only woman I've ever… The only woman I will ever… Please don't go. I'm begging you. It's all been for you. All this, all this everything. It's been for you. All the hard work, all the struggle. Been through a lot. You and me. And I'm nothing without you. Please… I will try harder. I'll try so hard to be good. To be better. All I want is to be good. Good for you, good for the kids. I want to get it right. You can teach me. Teach me to be kinder. I just want to get life right, to do the right thing by everyone and I know I've been messing up but it's so hard, isn't it? It's so bloody hard and Dad's gone now and I need you. I need you like you don't know. Please give me another chance. One more chance. Please…just…give me another chance. I'm really so, so sorry.

(*She looks at him for a time. She turns again to go, hesitates, turns back, watches him again. She then picks up her bags and slowly walks off. She stops outside and thinks.*

Alone, defeated, he sits.

After some time she returns inside. She watches him. She then walks slowly over to him. She stands over him as he sits. She then extends an arm and gently touches the back of his head.)

JANE: But you can't ever cry for me, can you? That's just something you can't ever actually do.

(*After a time she pulls his head towards her.*

He holds her tightly round the waist.)

SCENE 5

The present. JANE is sat at the table on the terrace, JIM stands close by. CATHY is preparing the bedroom, fighting her tears. WILLIAM and RICHARD are playing a tense game of chess in the living room, RICHARD struggling to stay with it.

WILLIAM: Wouldn't do that if I were you.
RICHARD: (*Replacing his chessman.*) I was just thinking…
    (*Outside:*)
JIM: It's a beautiful evening.
JANE: It really is.
    (*Inside:*)
RICHARD: (*To himself.*) Come on, come on, come on…
    (*In the bedroom, CATHY turns on a CD. It's of a Masai tribe singing. It's calming, serene. Only the singing for a time. Outside:*)
JIM: Do you still see the Wilsons?
JANE: From time to time.
JIM: And how are they?
JANE: They're both fine.
JIM: That's good.
    (*Inside:*)
WILLIAM: And I wouldn't do that if…
RICHARD: (*Replacing his chessman.*) I was just thinking…
    (*Only the singing for a time. Outside:*)
JANE: They're grandparents now.
JIM: That's lovely.
JANE: So they're both very pleased.
JIM: I'm sure they are.
JANE: Their eldest daughter's had twins.
JIM: It's hard to believe.
JANE: It really is.
JIM: They always seemed happy, the Wilsons.
JANE: I think they were. I think they are.
JIM: A happy couple.
JANE: Nice people.
    (*Only the singing for a time. Inside:*)
RICHARD: (*To himself.*) Come on, come on, come on…
    (*Only the singing for a time. Outside:*)

JIM: And you've got this grandson then?

JANE: Yes.

JIM: That's nice.

JANE: Don't see so much of him sadly.

JIM: That's a shame.

JANE: I'd hoped he was coming this weekend but…

JIM: Well, they do pick up things easily, the little ones.

JANE: It seems so.

(*Only the singing for a time.*)

Richard's wife is from Bangkok.

JIM: I gathered.

JANE: Never really speaks.

JIM: It's the land of smiles.

JANE: Sorry?

JIM: I said, it's the land of smiles.

JANE: (*After a pause.*) Yes.

(*Only the singing for a time. Inside:*)

RICHARD: There we go…

(*He makes a purposeful move on the chessboard. The music continues. Outside:*)

JANE: She's a lot younger than he is.

JIM: Really?

JANE: His wife. Thongbai. A lot younger.

JIM: That's nice…

JANE: Considerably younger.

(*Only the singing for a time. Inside WILLIAM makes a move.*)

JIM: Just as long as they're happy.

JANE: I do hope they are.

JIM: People have their ups and downs.

JANE: If we don't leave happy, peaceful children behind us when we go then…what on earth do we leave?

JIM: (*After a pause.*) Pots?

JANE: Yes. Pots. Better to leave lots and lots of lots of pots.

(*Only the singing for a time.*)

Jack's a delightful little boy.

JIM: Yes. I saw a photo. Inside. Very sweet.

JANE: But very small.

JIM: Well, I can imagine.

JANE: A little scrap of a thing.

(*Only the singing for a time. Inside:*)

RICHARD: Check!

WILLIAM: You can't do that, son.

RICHARD: Look, check!

WILLIAM: You can't move that. You move that piece, then you're in check yourself.

RICHARD studies the board.

It's an illegal move is that.

RICHARD reluctantly replaces his chessman.

(*Only the singing for a time. Outside:*)

JANE: His wife…Thongbai. She was a prostitute, you know. Last time he was here…he was drunk…as usual he was drunk…and I overheard him. On the phone. He clearly didn't remember saying it. In the morning.

JIM: I'm so sorry…

JANE: Oh, this drinking of his…this drinking…

JIM: I had no idea…

JANE: But I'm not pointing the finger. I suppose it's all that I've ever been. In a way.

(*Only the singing for a time. Inside:*)

RICHARD: (*To himself.*) Come on, Richard…

(*Only the singing for a time. Outside:*)

JANE: Given away my life for a little material comfort.

JIM: I can't bear to hear you say things like that.

JANE: I'm sorry…

JIM: I find that sort of thing quite difficult to hear.

(*Only the singing for a time.*)

JANE: It is very good of you to come.

JIM: I'm finding all this quite difficult.

(*Only the singing for a time. Inside RICHARD makes his move.*)

WILLIAM: Good move, son.

RICHARD: Thank you.

WILLIAM: Not a bad move at all.

RICHARD: Come on, come on, come on…

(*Only the singing for a time. Outside:*)

JANE: Were any of my Christmas cards forwarded to you?

JIM: They were, yes.

JANE: Twenty years of Christmas cards.

JIM: I received them.

JANE: And you never got in touch?

JIM: All I can say is we make our choices, Jane. We make our choices.

(Only the singing for a time. Inside WILLIAM is unsettled by RICHARD's last move. He rises and examines the board, sensing he is in trouble.

RICHARD pours himself a drink. The tension mounts.)

WILLIAM: Come on. Don't you think you've had enough now?

RICHARD: I'm almost forty.

WILLIAM: I beg your pardon?

RICHARD: I said, I'm almost forty.

(Only the singing for a time. Outside:)

JIM: I've been rehearsing a speech all the way down here in the car. But now I'm here…I really don't know what to say.

JANE: Well, I wanted to say sorry. For not coming with you. For not getting in touch. If he'd not come back early from his wretched conference that day, then I know I would have come but he did and so I stayed and I was wrong. I soon regretted it. But I should have had the courage to be alone. To leave him but be alone…

JIM: You could have been alone with me…

JANE: He's a good man. If I'd left then he would have been destroyed. I would have destroyed his life. My daughter would have managed…she's never needed anyone…but William would have been so lost.

JIM: He's a lucky man.

JANE: Women like me…we were bred to be loyal to our menfolk. Rather like dogs, I suppose. But we're all dying out now, thank the Lord. A dying breed of loyal little dogs…

JIM: Don't say that…

JANE: A dying breed of submissive little women.

(Only the singing for a time.)

JIM: You were the love of my life.

(Only the singing for a time.)

I never found anyone.

JANE: And I loved you. So much.

JIM: (*Walking away.*) Dear God, I can't bear this…

> (*Only the singing for a time. Inside WILLIAM now sits back at the chessboard. He sighs, scratches his head etc.*
> *RICHARD leans back semi-triumphantly and drinks.*
> *WILLIAM picks up a piece and is about to make his move.*)

RICHARD: If you let go of it, Dad…

WILLIAM: I know the rules.

RICHARD: …just remember there's no going back.

> (*WILLIAM eventually makes his move.*
> *In the bedroom CATHY is now placing numerous packets of pills on the bed.*
> *Only the Masai singing for a time. Outside:*)

JIM: London's not really me. I don't think I've ever found the right place. Places are either too large or too small.

JANE: But have you been at all happy?

JIM: (*After a pause.*) I'm happy in Jesus now.

JANE: Really?

JIM: The church is my family. This is yours.

> (*Only the singing for a time. Inside RICHARD stands.*)

RICHARD: I need the toilet.

WILLIAM: Go on then…

RICHARD: I know but…

WILLIAM: Go to the toilet then.

RICHARD: One time…one time you moved the pieces…

WILLIAM: Oh, don't be so daft…

RICHARD: One time you moved the pieces…

WILLIAM: The board simply got nudged.

RICHARD: Nudged? You knocked it over when …

WILLIAM: Listen, I am not going to touch this bloody board!

> (*RICHARD walks unsteadily off.*
> *WILLIAM watches him, sadly shaking his head.*
> *Only the Masai singing for a time. Outside:*)

JIM: Family is all there is. Who else is going to care for us if not family? But I have that now. So many good friends. And that's my family. Because you were the one…you were the one I…

JANE: Please…please, don't get upset…

(*Only the Masai singing for a time. Inside RICHARD returns.*
He walks back to the table.)

WILLIAM: Your move.

RICHARD: My move.

(*RICHARD sits and intensely studies the board.*
Only the Masai singing for a time. Outside:)

JANE: I do hope you can forgive me.

JIM: Of course.

(*Only the Masai singing for a time. Inside RICHARD makes a*
move.)

RICHARD: Check!

WILLIAM: Yes.

RICHARD: This time it is check, this time it is check, this time
it is check…

(*RICHARD stands, pacing in his excitement.*
Only the Masai singing for a time. Outside:)

JANE: I've wasted all my time, Jim.

JIM: No.

JANE: I was aware, when I was younger, that I was wasting
my time, that I was doing nothing with all this time but I
almost enjoyed wasting it. I thought if I looked after these
other people then that was something but look at them.
What has my care and my love done for any of them?

JIM: You mustn't say that.

(*Only the Masai singing for a time. Inside WILLIAM makes his*
move.
RICHARD anxiously returns to his chair.
WILLIAM now stands.
Outside JIM sits by JANE, his arm around her shoulder.)
None of us can know what's in store for us. We are
completely unable and unworthy to even think upon His
intentions. Trust me. God loves you.

(*Only the Masai singing for a time. Inside RICHARD makes*
his move.)

RICHARD: Check!

(*He leaps up again and paces.*
WILLIAM now sits again.

Only the Masai singing for a time. Outside:)

JANE: (*With a profound sadness, weariness.*) Why would He possibly want me to suffer like this?

JIM: We simply have to accept that He does.

JANE: I've tried to do no harm.

JIM: And you're a great woman.

JANE: But I should have stopped him... I should have protected...

(*Only the Masai singing for a time. Inside WILLIAM makes his move.*

RICHARD now over the board in intense concentration.

Both men standing, locking horns, as the song continues.

In the bedroom CATHY is arranging flowers in a vase. When she's done this, she sits on the bed and closes her eyes, meditating almost, listening to the song.

Eventually, still confident of imminent victory, RICHARD makes his move.

Both men with fixed stares at the board as the song continues.

Outside JIM closes his hands and his eyes in prayer.)

JIM: Most merciful God, Father of our Lord Jesus Christ, we confess that we have sinned in thought, word and deed.

(*JANE is now falling asleep in her wheelchair.*

CATHY turns off the music in the room and exits.

Inside WILLIAM makes his move.)

WILLIAM: Checkmate.

RICHARD: No!?

WILLIAM: Checkmate, I'm afraid.

(*Outside as the song continues and JANE sleeps on:*)

JIM: We have not loved you with our whole heart. We have not loved our neighbours as ourselves. In your mercy forgive what we have been, help us to amend what we are, and direct what we shall be; that we may do justly, love mercy, and walk humbly with you, our God. Amen.

(*As JIM looks up to see that JANE is asleep, inside RICHARD explodes into a rage. He kicks the board over and sends all the chess pieces flying.*)

RICHARD: (*Totally losing it.*) No fucking way!

WILLIAM: Steady on!

RICHARD: No fucking way!

WILLIAM: What the hell are you doing?

RICHARD: No way checkmate! No way checkmate!

WILLIAM: I had you pinned up against your own pawns! You didn't guard your back line!

RICHARD: No way checkmate! No way checkmate!

WILLIAM: This is a joke…

RICHARD: You didn't win, you didn't win….

WILLIAM: Oh just calm down.

RICHARD: I was winning, I know I was winning…

WILLIAM: Look, I won't take the money.

RICHARD: No way checkmate! No way checkmate!

WILLIAM: You're a drunk.

RICHARD: What did you say?

WILLIAM: A drunken disgrace…

RICHARD: Don't you say that to me…

(*RICHARD now grabs his father by the collar and yanks him towards him.*)

WILLIAM: Get off me!

RICHARD: Say that again!

WILLIAM: You're a drunken…disgrace.

RICHARD: You fucker! You great fat bullying fucker!

(*RICHARD pushes his father roughly and he falls onto his back.*)

Look at you now then! Just a sad old man.

WILLIAM: You've hurt my back.

RICHARD: Look at you…

WILLIAM: I said you've hurt my back.

RICHARD: All you do is talk! You talk and you talk and we all have to sit there listening. Well, we're not listening any more! Nobody's listening! And…you know what…I've been coming here for years! Just to see Mum. Years and years and you've been at the cricket and she's just never told you! What a marriage! What a great fucking marriage you have!

WILLIAM: Just help me.

(*At this point JIM comes in from outside.*)

JIM: Richard, Bill…this is of course none of my business but…

RICHARD: Your cosy middle-class life, your…

WILLIAM: There's nothing middle-class about me!

RICHARD: Just look around you…

WILLIAM: I worked bloody hard for this.

RICHARD: Your cricket club and your croquet on the lawn and your cafetières of coffee and your chess and your…

JIM: Please…

RICHARD: …little posh woman at the end of it all!

(JIM now helps WILLIAM to his feet.)

Your obedient little woman who never even loved you!

JIM: Now, that's not true…

RICHARD: It's all been for nothing!

WILLIAM: *(Moving towards him.)* Look around you, son! You think this is nothing? Never worked for a thing in your life. Just taken. Just taken from me. Taken from your mother. You're a scrounger and a disgrace! I've given you everything. I got you your job…

RICHARD: A shit job!

WILLIAM: I got you your house!

RICHARD: I don't want your house! I don't want your job! I don't want your life! I don't want your world!

WILLIAM: Well, that's tough, lad, because you're in it!

RICHARD: I hate my life!

WILLIAM: THEN BUGGER OFF BACK TO THAILAND AND LET'S SEE THE BLOODY BACK OF YOU THEN!

(A stunned silence.)

RICHARD: *(Tearful.)* I can't compete, I just can't ever…

WILLIAM: And take that bloody whore of a wife with you!

(A silence as RICHARD fully takes in what he's heard. He then suddenly lunges towards his father and a fight ensues. The two men roll around, knocking the sofa over etc. They wrestle, attempting to exchange body blows and eventually both are gripping each other round the neck. In the process of their struggle the pristine living room is turned into chaos.

CATHY now comes on.)

CATHY: What the hell are you doing?

(The fight continues.)

(*To JIM.*) What are they doing?

(*Eventually RICHARD is kneeling on his father's chest, pinning the man's arms to the floor.*)

RICHARD: Say Give! Say Give, sunbeam!

WILLIAM: (*Gasping for breath.*) Get off me!

RICHARD: Say Give, sunbeam! Just you say Give to me!

WILLIAM: Give, alright! Bloody give!

(*JANE has now wheeled herself into the room.*)

JANE: Get off him! Get off him now, you animal!

(*The company all stare at JANE.*)

That man is your father! He is your father and you will start respecting him. He's more of a man than you'll ever be! So, get off him! Get off him this instant!

(*RICHARD slowly gets off WILLIAM and moves away, his head down.*)

I can't believe what I'm seeing. My son, my husband…like children…like horrible little children. For God's sake, will someone please help him up?

(*JIM goes to WILLIAM and again tries to help him to his feet. This time his leg gives way and they both fall to the floor. CATHY now helps both men up.*)

I'm so tired.

CATHY: You help her to bed tonight, Dad.

JANE: (*To JIM.*) Goodnight.

JIM: Sweet dreams.

JANE: (*To RICHARD.*) And goodnight to you.

RICHARD: (*Embracing her.*) Sorry…

JANE: I've loved you so much. Remember that.

RICHARD: Sorry…

JANE: And you must stop drinking…

(*WILLIAM now wheels JANE off. Eventually they appear in the bedroom.*

A silence in the living room as JIM, CATHY and RICHARD survey the debris.)

JIM: Might be best for me to retire then?

CATHY: You know where your room is?

(*JIM looks to RICHARD. He touches his arm. He then exits.*)

A silence in both rooms. WILLIAM is helping his wife into bed from the wheelchair. CATHY starts clearing up the mess in the living room. After a time:)

RICHARD: I'm going home. Going home to see my son. See my little man, my little…son.
(He drunkenly walks off out of the room, across the terrace and exits as CATHY continues her work.
In the bedroom:)

WILLIAM: He just went for me. I beat him and you're right, the lad does need treatment. I'll pay for it, of course. Like we discussed.
(No response.
WILLIAM continues to make his wife comfortable while CATHY clears up in the living room.)
I know the man's always had a thing for you. I'm not completely daft but did you ever…love him back? It's okay. It's one of those things. I saw you once, you see. I thought that you two must have been… And I was working too much at that time and so… It's not so important. We all of us need our diversions. So maybe you've maybe had yours, and I think you've always suspected me of having mine…and there was a brief thing with…
(RICHARD reappears on the terrace and walks back towards the living room. He comes in.)

CATHY: You can't have them.

RICHARD: Want my keys.

CATHY: Go to bed.

RICHARD: Not sleeping in his house. Sleep in the car then… I'll just sleep in the car.
(He turns and staggers back across the terrace and then out.)

CATHY: *(To herself.)* The car he bought you…
(Back in the bedroom:)

JANE: You're wrong. Jim and I…we never…we never…

WILLIAM: You rest now…
(He gently kisses her on the forehead.)
You rest.
(We hear the car door slam off.)

EPILOGUE

The next morning. It's dull and raining. In the bedroom CATHY sits by the bed, in which JANE now lies dead. She is gently arranging her mother's hair. RICHARD comes on from the terrace, sober now but hungover again. He comes into the living room. He looks around and then walks to the piano. He opens it up. Hits a key. Then another. He begins playing the Bach from the opening of the play. His playing is not perfect but is certainly very good. After a time WILLIAM comes on unseen. He watches his son playing. He slowly gravitates towards the piano. He simply stands and listens. RICHARD finishes. A silence.

WILLIAM: Son?
> (*RICHARD looks round.*)
> That was…good. It was really very good.
> (*RICHARD stands.*
> *A silence as they stand next to each other.*)

RICHARD: Help me…
> (*WILLIAM does not respond.*)
> Please, Dad…will you please help me… I'm sorry. I'm so sorry for everything.
> (*WILLIAM slowly approaches his son.*
> *RICHARD then flings himself into his father's arms and holds him desperately. Soon RICHARD is sobbing into his father's chest.*)
> Can I come home, Dad? Please! Can I? Just for a while! Just for a little while, can I…

WILLIAM: Of course you can, son… Of course you bloody can…
> (*The embrace continues as JIM comes onto the terrace, with umbrella raised. He comes into the living room. He watches the two men. Then:*)

JIM: Just coming back from church and there's two policemen in the drive. They want to speak to you, Richard. I told them the delicacy of the situation here so they're kindly waiting back there for you.
> (*RICHARD breaks from the embrace. Then he slowly walks across the terrace and out.*)

WILLIAM: The police?
> (*CATHY now comes into the living room. A long silence.*)

CATHY: Mum's gone now. She's…flown away.

JIM: Flown away?

CATHY: Time for me to get on with my life now. Strange how happy I feel. How light. Dear Mum. She's written letters so hopefully…all will be well. And then, Dad, I'll be flying out to Mombassa. Don't know how long for. Two, three years. See a bit of the world while I'm still young. *Carpe diem* or whatever it's… Anyway…going for a sleep now. Yes. Going for a nice long sleep.

(*She exits and a silence falls in the room. JIM, stunned, slowly sits on the sofa. After a time he lets out a sob.*

WILLIAM, shocked and confused, watches the weeping man and is not sure what to do. He goes over to him and raises a hand as if to pat him on the back. He decides against it. He then leaves him there. He thinks. In his confusion he makes a move towards the bedroom, stops. Turns back into the room. He moves away and then looks outside at the rain. He walks out onto the terrace. He looks off to where his son's just departed and is about to follow.

A crow caws loudly from a tree.

WILLIAM stops.

Then it caws again.

WILLIAM looks out to his garden.

The bird again.

He continues to look out over his garden.)

www.ingramcontent.com/pod-product-compliance
Ingram Content Group UK Ltd.
Pitfield, Milton Keynes, MK11 3LW, UK
UKHW031251020325
455690UK00007B/95